# JAPAN AT WAR
## IN COLOR

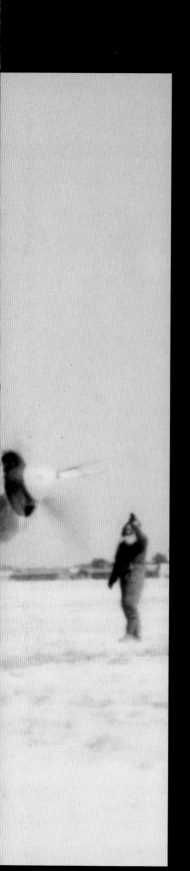

# JAPAN AT WAR

## IN COLOR

### David Batty

CARLTON

THIS IS A CARLTON BOOK

This edition first published in the US by
Carlton Books Ltd 2004
20 Mortimer Street
London W1T 3JW

First published in the UK by Carlton Books Ltd 2004.

Text copyright © 2004 TWI
Design copyright © 2004 Carlton Books Ltd

ISBN 1 84442 640 8

DEDICATION
For Jenny, Rosie and Amy

ACKNOWLEDGEMENTS
This book is an accompaniment to a 2-part television
series, JAPAN AT WAR IN COLOUR. My thanks go first
to all those at TWI and Carlton who made this all
possible. In particular, to Stewart Binns, Adrian Wood
and Alastair Waddington whose expertise and patience
knew no bounds; to Tricia Duffy, Zoe Payne and
Stephanie Burke for their tireless organisational skills;
and above all, to my film editor, Stephen Moore,
whose brilliance at editing and unfailing good humour,
allowed me to 'endure the unendurable'. In Tokyo,
thanks go to Miwa Komori of the TWI Office; and also
to my two researchers, Reiko Sakuma and Yukiko
Shimihara for their incredible hard work, unquestioning
devotion to the cause and cheery friendship. I also a
huge debt of inspiration to my father. But above all
else I want to thank my wife Jenny and two daughters,
Rosie and Amy, who had to cope on their own through
a very difficult year whilst I was away in Japan.
I would also like to thank Sodei Rinjiro for his kind
permission to quote from his excellent book, 'Dear
General MacArthur' (Maryland 2001).

Project Editors: Roland Hall & Gillian Holmes
Design: Karin Fremer, Diane Spender, Vicky Holmes
Production: Lisa Moore

Printed in Dubai

9 9 8 7 6 5 4 3 2

# CONTENTS

# INTRODUCTION

**D**ESPITE ITS RECENT ECONOMIC PROBLEMS, JAPAN IS STILL TODAY THE WORLD'S SECOND MOST POWERFUL ECONOMY, BEHIND ONLY ITS FORMER WARTIME ENEMY, THE UNITED STATES. YET JUST 150 YEARS AGO, IT WAS STILL A SEMI-FEUDAL STATE WITH A TINY ECONOMY, ISOLATED FROM THE REST OF THE WORLD. ITS ADVANCE TO WORLD POWER HAS BEEN BOTH DRAMATIC AND DESTRUCTIVE, AND INTERRUPTED IN 1945 BY CATASTROPHIC DISASTER – THE ONLY DEFEAT IN OVER 1000 YEARS OF HISTORY.

Central to this advance was the belief that the only way to prevent Japan's destruction as a nation was to emulate the powerful Western powers, both in terms of industrial and military might and also in imperial ambition. Japan's very survival depended on it becoming Asia's most powerful nation. Japan's leaders could clearly see that the rest of Asia was being carved up by the Western colonial nations and that Japan was next on the list. Its centuries-long isolation from the rest of the world could no longer be maintained and when it opened its doors, it was in danger of becoming the West's next imperial conquest. Almost from the start of this process Japan was on a collision course with the rest of the world. The Western powers' initial attempts to dominate Japan and their

later opposition to Japan's desire to join the imperial club helped create a deep-felt brooding resentment of Western interference and apparent hypocrisy. This helped spawn a host of increasingly extreme theories of revolutionary nationalism that helped hurl Japan into an attempted conquest of China and eventual disastrous confrontation with the West.

Japan's war didn't start at Pearl Harbor in 1941, it began almost ninety years before, when the West first came knocking on its doors. To understand Japan's decision to go to war against the Allies in 1941 and how it was prepared to fight almost to the death to avoid defeat, some knowledge of Japan's extraordinary history is needed. In particular how it transformed itself from a medieval to a modern nation.

# THE PATH TO POWER

ᴇᴀʀʟʏ ɴɪɴᴇᴛᴇᴇɴᴛʜ-ᴄᴇɴᴛᴜʀʏ Jᴀᴘᴀɴ ᴡᴀꜱ ᴀ ᴡᴏʀʟᴅ ᴀᴘᴀʀᴛ. Iꜱᴏʟᴀᴛᴇᴅ ꜰʀᴏᴍ ᴀʟʟ ᴏᴜᴛꜱɪᴅᴇ ᴄᴏɴᴛᴀᴄᴛ, Jᴀᴘᴀɴ ᴡᴀꜱ ᴀ ɴᴀᴛɪᴏɴ ʀᴜʟᴇᴅ ʙʏ ᴀ ᴍɪʟɪᴛᴀʀʏ ᴅɪᴄᴛᴀᴛᴏʀ, ᴛʜᴇ Sʜᴏɢᴜɴ, ʜɪꜱ ᴅᴀɪᴍʏᴏ ᴡᴀʀʟᴏʀᴅꜱ ᴀɴᴅ ᴛʜᴇɪʀ ꜱᴀᴍᴜʀᴀɪ ꜰᴏʟʟᴏᴡᴇʀꜱ. Tʀᴀᴅɪᴛɪᴏɴ ᴅᴇᴍᴀɴᴅᴇᴅ ᴛʜᴀᴛ ᴛʜᴇ ꜱᴀᴍᴜʀᴀɪ ꜰᴏʟʟᴏᴡᴇᴅ ᴛʜᴇɪʀ ᴍᴇᴅɪᴇᴠᴀʟ ᴄᴏᴅᴇ ᴏꜰ ʜᴏɴᴏᴜʀ ᴀɴᴅ ᴍᴏʀᴀʟꜱ ᴋɴᴏᴡɴ ᴀꜱ ʙᴜꜱʜɪᴅᴏ. Fᴏʀ ᴛʜᴇ ꜱᴀᴍᴜʀᴀɪ ꜱᴜᴄʜ ᴘᴇʀꜱᴏɴᴀʟ ǫᴜᴀʟɪᴛɪᴇꜱ ᴀꜱ ʟᴏʏᴀʟᴛʏ, ʜᴏɴᴏᴜʀ, ᴄᴏᴜʀᴀɢᴇ ᴀɴᴅ ꜱᴇʟꜰ-ᴅᴇɴɪᴀʟ ᴡᴇʀᴇ ᴘᴀʀᴀᴍᴏᴜɴᴛ. Hɪꜱ ᴋᴇʏ ꜱʏᴍʙᴏʟꜱ ᴡᴇʀᴇ ᴛʜᴇ ꜱᴡᴏʀᴅ, ᴡʜɪᴄʜ ʀᴇᴘʀᴇꜱᴇɴᴛᴇᴅ ʜɪꜱ ꜱᴏᴜʟ; ᴀɴᴅ ᴛʜᴇ ᴄʜᴇʀʀʏ ᴛʀᴇᴇ, ᴡʜᴏꜱᴇ ʙʟᴏꜱꜱᴏᴍꜱ ᴅʀᴏᴘ ᴀᴛ ᴛʜᴇ ꜰɪʀꜱᴛ ʙʀᴇᴀᴛʜ ᴏꜰ ᴡɪɴᴅ, ᴊᴜꜱᴛ ᴀꜱ ᴛʜᴇ ꜱᴀᴍᴜʀᴀɪ ᴡᴏᴜʟᴅ ᴅɪᴇ ꜰᴏʀ ʜɪꜱ ʟᴏʀᴅ ᴡɪᴛʜᴏᴜᴛ ǫᴜᴇꜱᴛɪᴏɴ. Hɪꜱ ʟɪꜰᴇ ᴡᴀꜱ ᴇxᴘᴇᴄᴛᴇᴅ ᴛᴏ ʙᴇ ᴏɴᴇ ᴏꜰ ᴘʜʏꜱɪᴄᴀʟ ʜᴀʀᴅꜱʜɪᴘ; ʟᴜxᴜʀʏ ᴡᴀꜱ ꜱᴇᴇɴ ᴀꜱ ᴀ ᴡᴇᴀᴋɴᴇꜱꜱ. Rɪᴛᴜᴀʟ ꜱᴜɪᴄɪᴅᴇ ᴡᴀꜱ ᴀɴ ᴀᴄᴄᴇᴘᴛᴇᴅ ᴍᴇᴛʜᴏᴅ ᴏꜰ ʀᴇꜱᴏʟᴠɪɴɢ ᴅɪꜰꜰɪᴄᴜʟᴛɪᴇꜱ ɪɴᴠᴏʟᴠɪɴɢ ʜᴏɴᴏᴜʀ ᴀɴᴅ ᴡᴀꜱ ᴅᴏɴᴇ ʙʏ ꜱᴇᴘᴘᴜᴋᴜ – ᴀ ᴘᴀɪɴꜰᴜʟ ᴅᴇᴀᴛʜ ʙʏ ᴅɪꜱᴇᴍʙᴏᴡᴇʟʟɪɴɢ.

By the nineteenth century, shoguns had ruled Japan for almost 700 years, with the emperor as a mere symbol. Since the late sixteenth century one family had dominated, the Tokugawas. For hundreds of years, European merchants had been trying to establish regular trade links with Japan, but the Tokugawas had prohibited virtually all contact with the outside world. Ocean-going ships were prohibited and any Japanese who left the country was forbidden to return, or risked execution. Trade with Europeans was restricted to a single trading post run by the Dutch on a tiny island in Nagasaki harbour, on the southern island of Kyushu. The importing of European culture was very limited, especially books, and any form of Christian literature

was banned under pain of death. Using such strictly isolationist policies the Tokugawa shoguns had succeeded in protecting Japan from colonization by the west and had maintained a relatively prosperous economy. It was the longest period of uninterrupted peace Japan ever enjoyed.

Behind these barriers Japanese society was organized in a strict hierarchy of classes. At the top were the bushi or nobility, consisting of the daimyo and samurai; below them came the peasants, making up more than three quarters of the population; below them again came the craftsmen; and right at the bottom of the social ladder were the merchants. Those who used commerce as their prime means of support were seen almost as outcasts in Japanese society, much like the Jews of medieval Europe. Life in Tokugawa Japan depended on exploitation of the peasants by the nobility. Village life was highly organized and conformist. Everyone knew his place in the order of things. It was the responsibility of the village headman – who had usually inherited his position – to ensure that the village's taxes were paid and that the local daimyo's laws were kept. The Tokugawa shoguns had revived the ancient Chinese administrative system by which village households were divided into groups of five men or pao, each of whom was held responsible for the conduct of the others. Through this system almost every important aspect of life was controlled including marriage, inheritance and succession.

OPPOSITE PAGE: A GROUP OF JAPANESE FARMERS, C.1870S.
ABOVE: A MAN SELLING FUTONS, C.1870S.

The regime of the Tokugawas had provided the Japanese people with a largely peaceful environment in which to prosper, both economically and culturally, but by the early nineteenth century there were many internal tensions. An overblown and increasingly corrupt bureaucracy, a hierarchical class system that no longer reflected the economic realities of life and a series of famines and natural disasters all combined to create a sense of crisis. Some people called for even more restrictions on foreigners and outside contacts, the rooting out of luxury amongst the ruling class and a return to the old ways of the samurai. Others demanded an end to the Shogun and a return to Imperial rule. Tokugawa Japan was on its last legs.

While Japan had kept its doors closed, the rest of the world had thrown them open. By the mid-nineteenth century the process of unifying the world into a single capitalist system was gathering pace. The West's merchant fleets had already been exploiting large parts of the globe for hundreds of years and were always on the hunt for new markets. Japan could not resist this onslaught for ever; it was only a question of time before it would have to deal with European and American traders and their governments. For Japan's leaders, the question was now not whether Japan should enter the global system, but how. An indication of what they might expect could be seen on the Asian continent. There the Western powers had gained access to China by force and were plundering its resources for their own benefit. Japan's leaders feared that Japan's entry into the modern world could threaten its very survival as an independent state.

All around the Pacific, the capitalist system was closing in. Russia controlled Siberia and was colonizing Alaska. The British had trading concessions on the Chinese mainland and were keen to win port rights in Japan. Across the Pacific to the east, the United States was rapidly expanding its frontiers. In 1851, a second gold rush began in Australia, to Japan's south, while the newly formed Pacific Mail Steamship Company was planning a regular

route from San Francisco to Shanghai – a route that would take steamships close to the Japanese coastline. The American whaling industry was now operating throughout the Pacific. Japan was surrounded by a world dominated by the Western powers with their irresistible economic and military might.

In 1853 the US government sent a squadron of four warships under Commodore Matthew Perry with instructions to use force if necessary to open diplomatic relations with Japan. On July 8 Perry's ships, including some of the US Navy's most modern steam-powered warships, anchored in Edo Bay. Never before had the

A woman carrying firewood, c.1870s.

Japanese seen ships steaming with smoke. They described them as "giant dragons puffing smoke" and the "Black Ships". They were particularly impressed by the number and size of the cannons the ships carried.

There had been several previous abortive American attempts to open trade with Japan. In 1837 an unarmed ship, the *Morrison*, had tried to enter Edo Bay but had been fired on by Japanese shore batteries. Nine years later a second US Navy expedition, commanded by Commodore Biddle, again entered Edo Bay, but Biddle proved a poor negotiator and his mission also failed. Just a year later, in 1847, a third expedition under Commander Glyn in the USS *Preble*, sailed into Nagasaki harbour in the south. Despite threats of force, negotiations again broke down and Glyn left empty-handed.

It was against this background of failure that the US Congress had dispatched Commodore Perry to Japan. Perry had been given three

COMMODORE PERRY ARRIVES IN JAPAN IN 1854 TO SIGN THE TREATY OF KANAGAWA.

aims: to ensure the future good treatment of American castaways in Japan; to secure the use of one or more ports for supplies and fuel for American ships; and above all to open Japan for trade. And he was, of course, to ensure that America be given a dominant position in this new trading relationship.

The commodore was determined to make a success of the mission. He had researched extensively into Japan and gathered experts in various fields to join the expedition. The renowned German painter William Heine was appointed official artist. Eliphalet M. Brown, a talented young daguerreotypist, was asked to join the expedition as its official photographer. The US State Department provided an agricultural specialist and botanist, Dr James Morrow. Perry also found an Asian expert, S. Wells Williams, who had been to Japan in 1837, to act as his interpreter.

Perry already had a long and distinguished career in the US Navy behind him but his mission to Japan would be his most significant accomplishment. Learning from the failure of previous missions he refused to allow his vessels to be surrounded by Japanese boats. He brought a letter from the President of the United States, Millard Fillmore, to the Emperor of Japan, and he refused to negotiate with anyone who was not of the highest rank. After presenting his credentials and the letter from the American president with great pomp and ceremony, Perry left Japan promising to return a year later for an answer.

The shogun and his advisers were thrown into turmoil by this new aggressive approach from the United States. Lord Abe, the chief counsellor to the shogun asked members of the government for advice. The reply from the Prince of Mito summed up the mood: "The barbarians have been watching our country with greedy eyes for many years ... if now we resort to a wilfully dilatory method of procedure, we shall gnaw our navels afterward when it will be of no use."

The Meiji Restoration did not mean that the emperor ruled directly; rather he was expected to accept the advice of the group of powerful men which had overthrown the shogun. It was from this group that a small number of ambitious, able and patriotic young men, mostly from the lower ranks of the old samurai class, emerged to take control and establish a new political system. They moved quickly to reinforce military and economic control and within three years had forced the daimyo warlords to give up their feudal lands and had replaced them with the prefectures of a unified central state.

The daimyo and samurai were paid off and their class privileges abolished. By 1876 the government had banned the carrying of swords and former samurai were being encouraged to cut off their traditional topknots in favour of Western-style haircuts and to take up business and the professions. The warlord's private armies were disbanded, and a national army based on universal conscription was created in 1872, requiring three years' military service from all adult males. A centralized taxation system was also established which required payment in money instead of rice, allowing the government to stabilize the national budget and create the finance needed to invest in the nation's infrastructure.

In an attempt to unite the Japanese nation in response to the challenge of the West, a new state ideology was promoted centred on the emperor. He had always stood as a symbol of Japanese culture and a direct link to the past. He was also the chief priest of Shinto, Japan's native religion. All followers of Shinto believed that the emperor was directly descended from the gods who had created Japan and therefore he himself was divine, a living god. The emperor was rarely seen, but when he did appear, people were now required to prostrate themselves and cover their eyes. Above all, everyone was expected to carry out the emperor's orders without question or comment. He became a powerful symbol of national unity and his authority would provide an effective means of state control during both peace and war.

The abrupt abolition of feudalism caused a social and political earthquake in Japan. Millions of people were suddenly free to choose their occupations and move about without restrictions. The government led the way by investing in new industries, building railway and shipping lines, telegraph and telephone systems, shipyards, mines, armaments factories and countless other factories. This was a very costly process and put enormous pressure on the government's finances, so in 1880 it was decided to sell most of these new industries to private individuals, with generous subsidies and other incentives to encourage continued investment. As a result, some of the most famous names in Japanese industry and world trade were born, Mitsubishi, Mitsui and Sumitomo amongst others. Based around webs of family connections, vast and largely unchecked economic empires known as *zaibatsu* were created, that would later wield huge economic and political power and play a major role in Japan's imperial ambitions both at home and abroad.

In 1872 a national system of education was established, and by the end of the century almost everyone was attending publicly funded schools for at least six years. The government closely controlled the school curriculum, ensuring that in addition to essential skills such as mathematics and reading, all students also had substantial "moral training" which stressed the importance of their duty to the emperor, the country and their families. In 1889 the emperor granted his people a constitution, but from the start it was made clear that only he or his close advisers could change it. This was no democratic revolution but more a piece of authoritarian window dressing. A parliament was duly elected in 1890, but only a tiny proportion of the population was given the vote. In 1925 the vote was extended to all adult males but women would have to wait until 1946 before they were allowed to participate in politics.

In 1894 Japan fought its first war as a modern state, against China, over its interests in the Korean peninsula. Korea is the closest part of the Asian land mass to Japan, less than 100 miles by sea, and the Japanese were concerned that the Russians might gain control of it. Japan won the war and took effective control of Korea, in addition gaining Taiwan as a colony. This decisive victory surprised the world and provided the European powers with a warning of Japan's growing strength. Around this time the European nations were beginning to claim "special rights" in China. The French, from their colony in Indochina (today's Vietnam, Laos and Cambodia) were extending their influence into southern China. The British also claimed special influence in the south, around Hong Kong, and later along the whole Yangtze valley. The Russians were building a railway through Siberia and Manchuria and so were interested in northern China. Japan was an unwelcome newcomer with its new presence in Korea and the Liaodong peninsula and the colony in Taiwan.

CROWDS IN TOKYO CELEBRATE THE END OF THE JAPAN-CHINA WAR, 1895.

France, Russia and Germany were soon pressuring China to cede them ports, naval bases and special economic privileges and to deny Japan its newly won rights. In time Japan was compelled to hand back control of the Liaodong peninsula to the Chinese. It was a stark lesson for Japan in the realities of late nineteenth-century realpolitik and its leaders resolved to strengthen the military even further. So by 1904, when the Russians were again threatening to establish control over Korea, Japan's army and navy were much bigger and stronger, and it felt able to take on a fully fledged Western military power. After a series of stunning victories, including a surprise naval attack against the Russian fleet at Port Arthur, Japan was again victorious. It had finally achieved undisputed control of Korea, thereby establishing itself as a significant colonial power in East Asia.

On the early twentieth-century world stage, Japan's chief handicap was that it was an Asian nation. The colonialism, and the racism that accompanied it, were too entrenched in Western countries to allow an upstart non-white nation to enter the race for natural resources and markets on an equal basis. Much of the future friction between the West and Japan stemmed from this sense of alienation. The Western Powers appeared to adopt different standards in dealing with Japan and so its military leaders increasingly felt that the country's security depended on controlling both the land and the sea that surrounded it. This, of course, meant an ever bigger army and navy and created a situation with great potential for future conflict.

THE JAPANESE IMPERIAL GUARDS ATTACK THE RUSSIAN POSITIONS AT KOWLIANG IN JULY, 1905.

THE MEIJI EMPEROR REVIEWS 160 WARSHIPS OF THE IMPERIAL NAVY.

One significant result of the Russo-Japanese war was growing enmity between Japan and the USA. The US president had brokered the peace between a desperate Russia and an exhausted Japan and although as victors the Japanese got most of what they wanted, they went away disappointed they did not receive even more. Back in Japan the public was so angry that there were widespread demands for the resignation of the government. Newspapers claimed the politicians had managed to turn a military success into a political defeat. There were riots in Tokyo and the government declared martial law. To get themselves off the hook the politicians blamed the Americans and ill-feeling between the two nations grew.

On the Japanese side resentment at the one-sided nature of the treaty of 1854 had persisted, while in the United States the last decades of the nineteenth century had seen growing anti-Japanese sentiment, a racist reaction to the increasing numbers of poor Japanese immigrants who came to the USA looking for work. The American press pandered to public fears of this "yellow peril". The *San Francisco Chronicle* used headlines such as "Japanese a Menace to American Women" and "Brown Asiatics Steal Brains of Whites". The California legislature voted unanimously to demand that Congress exclude all Japanese and the newly formed Japanese and Korean Exclusion League enrolled thousands of new members. In Japan, the newspapers demanded that Admiral Togo send a fleet of warships to teach the Americans a lesson, and Togo and his fellow naval officers concluded that, since the defeat of Russia, the United States now represented the prime threat to Japan.

Meanwhile, the quest for empire continued. In the summer of 1905, Korea was made a protectorate but Japan was looking for a pretext to annex the peninsula outright. This came in October 1909, when a senior Japanese statesman, Prince Itoh, was assassinated in Harbin in north-east China. A Korean nationalist was arrested and charged with his murder. Although almost certainly a put-up job, it was all the excuse the Japanese government needed to take over completely. Less than 50 years after the Meiji Restoration, Japan had an empire stretching from Taiwan in the south to Korea in the west and Sakhalin in the north, encompassing the Ryukyu Islands, the Bonins and the Kuriles.

In 1912 the Meiji Emperor died at the age of 60, leaving a son who was in no way fit to rule Japan. The new emperor was optimistically named Taisho (Great Righteousness) but his reign was plagued by political rivalry and instability that damaged the prestige of the throne. Emperor Taisho was so physically weak and mentally incapable that the entire function of government fell into the hands of the small group of military and political advisers around the throne. So began a power struggle that was to define Japan's next quarter of a century and would see a gradual replacement of civil by military authority. A key factor in this is that under the constitution of 1889, the military enjoyed what was defined as "the independence of the Supreme Command". This meant that neither the Diet (the Japanese Parliament) nor the Cabinet had any authority over them. They were only answerable to the Emperor himself. As time went on, the military felt increasingly independent of civilian control.

At the outbreak of the First World War in 1914, Japan joined the Allies against Germany. Japan contributed little to the Allied cause other than taking the opportunity to extend its empire by seizing the German colonies in Asia – Jiaozhou Bay in China and the Mariana, Marshall and Caroline Islands in the Pacific. Japanese nationalists argued that as the Western powers were fully occupied with the war in Europe, now was the time to move into China, so, after presenting an impossible set of demands to the Chinese, the Japanese mobilized their forces. The Chinese government quickly capitulated and the Japanese moved into Manchuria and Outer Mongolia and also established a substantial military presence in Shanghai. Following the Russian collapse after the Bolshevik revolution in 1917, Japan also sent a large force into Siberia. When the First World War finally ended, the Japanese had a lot to bargain with at the Paris Peace Conference.

JAPANESE PLANES BOMBARD THE RUSSIAN POSITIONS AT KIAOCHOW BAY, DURING THE RUSSO-JAPANESE WAR, 1905.

The Versailles treaty gave Japan virtually all it asked for in China and the Pacific. Japanese troops remained in Siberia until 1922, the last Allied forces to leave Soviet Russia, and occupied northern Sakhalin until 1926. Now that it had joined the colonial powers in pursuit of territory and prestige, Japan wanted to be treated as an equal in international dealings but the Americans did all they could to prevent Japanese expansion, especially in China. The Japanese resented this

A JAPANESE WOMAN'S 'VICTORY POEM' TO HER LOVER, 1905.

A POSTCARD CELEBRATING JAPAN'S NEW STATUS AS A WORLD POWER, 1905.

continued American discrimination. They were especially angry at the American veto of a Japanese-sponsored move to include a "racial equality" clause in the Versailles peace treaty. Relations between the two countries became increasingly difficult. Just as the Japanese military had begun to view the United States as its major potential enemy, the growth of Japanese naval power worried the government in Washington.

During the winter of 1921–2, an international conference was held in the US capital, attended by those nations with interests in the Pacific and Asia, including Britain, France, the Netherlands, Portugal, Italy and China. The Japanese government did not yet feel strong enough to defy world opinion, so decided to participate. The conference agreed that all nations should have equal rights to engage in trade and commerce in China, but Japan was forced to return to China the former German territory of Shandong and to withdraw its forces from northern China. Most importantly, the size of each nation's navy was fixed, with Japan only being permitted three major warships for every five for Britain and the United States. It was a major blow to Japan's international prestige but one it was not yet powerful enough to challenge. In the eyes of the Western powers, Japan was still a second-class power and they intended to keep the Japanese in their place.

The results of the conference were deeply unpopular in Japan. They were seen as a humiliation, especially the limits placed on the navy. The chief of the Japanese naval board was so upset that he announced that a "war" had already begun between the United States and Japan. The consequences of the deal within Japan were to damage the reputation of politicians and to shift influence towards the military, especially the more extreme elements who wanted Japan to continue its expansion into Asia.

A TRADITIONAL NEW YEAR CARD FROM CAPTAIN IWAO OYAMA SERVING IN CHINA, c1920s.

By the end of the First World War, the Japanese economy had almost tripled in output since the late nineteenth century. Commerce had risen by 180%, mining and manufacturing by 580% and transport, communications and public utilities by over 1700%. The expansion of empire meant growth in markets for industrial goods. Imperialism was good for business. But industrialization also introduced radical political ideas and trade unions. By the early 1920s, union organizers and radicals were leading strikes and disturbances. The government responded with repressive legislation.

The basic instrument of state control was the Peace Preservation Law, first passed in 1887 with several revisions over the years. By the early 1920s, the law provided for the suppression of anything that threatened "peace and order". It was routinely used to quell riots, to put down demonstrations, to control trade union activity and any radical political action. It operated through an efficient and widespread police network. There was a *koban* or police box on every street corner in every locality throughout Japan. These served as both a highly effective intelligence-gathering organization and as a direct means of social control. The police knew everyone, where they lived and what they were up to. People even bowed to the *koban* as they passed in the street. The foundations for a police state were already being laid.

By the late 1920s, the world was slipping into a massive recession and Japan would not escape its effects. The Japanese economy, particularly its agricultural sector, was shattered by the Great Depression. One Japanese journalist wrote in the *New York Times* in 1931 how the world depression had struck Japan "a staggering blow and has profoundly affected the mental outlook of the entire nation ... A pall of gloom has been cast about the people." Two examples show the scale of the tragedy. Rice prices slumped by a third between 1929 and 1930, and for many of Japan's small farmers – the largest proportion of the rural population – this meant economic ruin. Silk prices, the other mainstay of the rural economy, dropped by more than 50 per cent. Combined with a population explosion, these price collapses led to widespread malnutrition, starvation and even reports of cannibalism and suicide. Many families resorted to the ancient custom of selling daughters into prostitution to reduce the numbers of mouths to feed and produce extra income.

Despite modernization and industrialization, Japan was still a rural nation at heart and the majority of the army and navy, both officers and men, came from rural districts; military service was one of the few ways to escape rural poverty. So when soldiers returned from leave with ever more desperate stories of misery at home, anger within the armed forces at the economic situation grew. The military's rage was largely directed against politicians and the parliamentary system which had apparently failed Japan's rural masses, and fostered the growth of myriad ultra-nationalist secret societies. The Japanese became increasingly disenchanted with Western-inspired ideas of constitutional monarchy and more drawn to an authoritarian, militaristic future.

THE DISTRICT OF KUDANSHITA IN TOKYO IN THE 1920s.

JAPANESE GENERAL NOGI (MIDDLE ROW, SECOND FROM LEFT) AND RUSSIAN GENERAL STOSSEL (ON NOGI'S LEFT) MEET AFTER RUSSIAN SURRENDER, JANUARY 1905.

Patriotic societies had always been popular in Japan. Many of them operated secretly and had supporters in high positions in both military and civil circles. The Black Ocean Society was formed in 1880 with the motto, "Honour the imperial family, respect the empire and guard the rights of the people". It ran an extensive network of spies all over Asia and waged a terror campaign that culminated in the murder of Queen Min of Korea in 1895. The Black Dragon or River Amur Society was founded in 1901. Its membership quickly grew into thousands and included high-ranking military officers and even members of the cabinet. The Cherry Blossom Society was begun in the late 1920s by a group of army officers to promote colonial expansion in Asia. Another society, The Foundation of the State, set up by General Araki, a senior army officer and war minister, popularized the notion of *Kodo* or the Imperial Way, linking emperor, people, land and morality in one indivisible totalitarian whole. *Kodo* emphasized emperor worship through Shintoism and "spiritual training" for the army.

Like Europe's emerging fascist parties, Japanese patriotic societies eschewed class struggle in favour of national unity.

Some of them even disagreed with the very existence of an elected parliament. Most preached against what they saw as the corrupting influence of money and industrialization. All of them were prepared to use physical violence to further their cause.

From the late 1920s, Japan entered an era of government by coup and assassination, as more extreme elements began to make their presence felt. Increasing violence and weak governments led to growing military influence over civil affairs. Much of this political activity centred on Japan's Kwantung army based in Asia, whose commanders pursued progressively more independent policies to ensure Japanese domination of the Manchurian province of China. In 1928, officers in the Kwantung army arranged the murder of a Chinese warlord as the pretext for an increased military presence in Manchuria. The government in Tokyo proved powerless to prevent such activities. Even when army officers were disciplined the punishments were minimal. The parliamentarians were rapidly losing control of Japan's future.

# MANCHUKUO

# Chapter 2

BY THE EARLY 1930S, JAPAN'S MOST PRESSING FOREIGN POLICY ISSUE WAS CHINA. THERE WAS GROWING DOMESTIC SUPPORT FOR THE IDEA THAT JAPAN SHOULD OCCUPY THE DOMINANT POSITION IN ASIA, THAT IT SHOULD REPLACE THE OLD WHITE COLONIAL POWERS AS ASIA'S LEADING POWER. THE QUESTION WAS HOW THIS COULD BE ACHIEVED, BY PEACEFUL MEANS OR THROUGH MILITARY CONQUEST. IN 1931 JAPAN'S MAIN OVERSEAS POSSESSIONS WERE KOREA AND TAIWAN BUT IT ALSO HAD A SIGNIFICANT PRESENCE IN CHINA. IT WAS FAST BECOMING A COMPARABLE COLONIAL POWER TO BRITAIN, THE NETHERLANDS, FRANCE AND THE UNITED STATES. BUT PARITY WAS NOT THE AIM; JAPAN WANTED TO DOMINATE. THROUGH A NUMBER OF INCREASINGLY SERIOUS INCIDENTS WHOSE TRUE CAUSES ARE NOW LOST, JAPAN WAS TO EXTEND ITS INFLUENCE IN ASIA TO THE POINT OF CONFRONTATION WITH THE REST OF THE WORLD.

The first point of conflict was provided by the Chinese province of Manchuria. For some years Japan had regarded Manchuria as its exclusive sphere of influence. It was seen as vital to Japan's economic well-being as it provided oil, coal, iron and foodstuffs such as soya beans, resources that Japan itself lacked. Japanese business had invested heavily in the province, and by the early 1930s there were over 800 Japanese-owned factories, but Manchuria was still not officially part of the Japanese empire; it was a province in the vast and increasingly chaotic nation of China, fought over by warlords, nationalists and communists. An influential group of Japanese men, mainly in the military, believed that Japanese control over Manchuria should be made secure and permanent.

At first control was extended by peaceful means. Government incentives were made available to Koreans and Japanese in the form of low-interest loans for the purchase of land, to encourage them to emigrate. Relatively few Japanese took up the offer but Koreans flooded in. This caused much resentment among the Manchurian and Chinese population, and in the summer of 1931 this boiled over into violence when a group of Koreans confronted Chinese farmers over some disputed land at Wanpaoshan. The Koreans called for help from Japanese police guarding the local consulate. They fired on the Chinese and drove them off. In June a Japanese army officer, Captain Nakamura, was arrested by Chinese troops in Mongolia. He was searched, a suspicious map was found and he was summarily shot as a spy. When news of his killing got out, a huge diplomatic row erupted. The Chinese government tried to resolve the matter peacefully but there was much support in Japan for retribution, particularly among military leaders and extremists who were looking for an excuse to invade Manchuria and integrate it fully into the empire.

By this stage, the Kwantung army was operating almost independently of the government in Japan. Many of its key officers belonged to secret societies and believed that the army was an instrument of divine salvation with a mission to bring Japanese civilization to the world through military conquest. Manchuria was key to this vision as a source of the raw materials needed for this future global conflict. On the night of September 18, 1931, a section of the railway just north of the major city of Mukden (Shenyang) in Manchuria was blown up and the explosion blamed on the Chinese. The Kwantung army immediately went on the offensive and captured Mukden and a number of other strategic towns in the area.

The consequences of the Mukden Incident, as it became known, reverberated around the world. While the Kwantung army demanded reinforcements, the Chinese government asked the League of Nations for support. Back in Tokyo, the government faced a *fait accompli*. As the politicians lacked both the will and the power to oppose the army's actions, they authorized the sending of more troops. When the emperor was consulted (Hirohito had succeeded in 1926) his attitude was one of reluctant acceptance. Everyone in the government knew the incident had been staged by the army, but as it had been a success they were prepared to go along with it.

In Geneva, under American pressure, the League of Nations invoked the Kellogg–Briand Pact of 1928 which had renounced war and which both Japan and China had signed. Despite Japanese opposition, the league agreed on a deadline of November 16 for a total Japanese withdrawal from occupied areas in Manchuria, but when the deadline passed and the Japanese still refused to withdraw, the league did nothing to make them comply. The major powers had other more pressing worries to attend to with the continuing disastrous effects of the Great Depression. In any case, a powerful Japan might just provide a buffer against the growing threat of communist Russia. The best the league could do was send a commission to Manchuria to report back on the situation.

ABOVE: JAPANESE TROOPS FIGHTING IN CHINA IN 1930S.
OVERLEAF: JAPANESE HORSE ARTILLERY IN CHINA IN 1930S.

JAPANESE MACHINE GUN CREW IN THE ADVANCE ON NANKING 1937.

In Japan, the invasion of Manchuria gained huge support in the press. There were large public rallies and campaigns were started to raise money to buy military equipment. The Kwantung army ran a very effective propaganda machine through sympathetic retired army officers. Their arguments for a permanent occupation of Manchuria – self-defence and to prevent a Communist Russian invasion – struck a chord in Japan.

In December 1931, a new government came to power in Tokyo led by the nationalist Tsuyoshi Inukai. He had come out in favour of the Manchurian occupation and in response to the League of Nations' criticisms, declared that Japan "should escape from the diplomacy of apology [and develop] a new, more autonomous road". One of the most powerful positions in the cabinet was that of the war minister, an appointment that had to be approved by the army high command. The new appointee was General Sadao Araki, an ultra-nationalist. He had helped to revive the wearing of samurai swords by army officers and advocated committing suicide rather than surrendering. He was a determined proponent of Japan's sacred mission to dominate first Asia and then the world. To do this he believed

Japan had first to adopt the way of the soldier and become a fully militaristic state. For his supporters, Araki was the ultimate hero and an ominous sign of things to come.

By the beginning of 1932, the Kwantung army was in full control of Manchuria, but the fighting did not stop there. At the end of January, after growing hostility towards Japanese interests in China and more incidents involving Japanese residents, the consul-general in Shanghai demanded something be done. This time it was the navy that acted. On the night of January 28, 1932, 2,000 Japanese marines attacked the Chinese army in the Chapei district of Shanghai. The fighting was savage and many atrocities were committed on the Chinese population, acts that would later become routine in the Japanese invasion and occupation of China. Naval aircraft were called in, the first major example of the bombing of civilians from the air. Casualties on both sides were high but the Chinese refused to give in and the fighting escalated. Reinforcements from the Japanese army were sent in, including tanks and heavy artillery, and eventually the Chinese were forced to retreat.

The Japanese press featured many stories of heroism from the fighting at Shanghai; one favourite was that of an officer from the army's Ninth Infantry Division. He had been left seriously wounded on the battlefield when his unit retreated. The Chinese captured him and treated his wounds. He then returned to the spot where he had been wounded and committed seppuku to prove his dedication to the imperial cause. Another report related how three Japanese soldiers had tied explosives to their bodies and then hurled themselves at a Chinese bunker, killing everyone inside. The nationalists used stories like these to illustrate the sort of moral fibre required of both the Japanese soldier and civilian: death before surrender and a willingness to die for the cause.

JAPANESE MARINES HONOUR THEIR FALLEN COMRADES OUTSIDE SHANGHAI, 1932.

In February, Japanese-occupied Manchuria was transformed into the "independent" country of Manchukuo with its capital and government at Changchun. Despite the presence of one Manchurian, one Mongolian and three Chinese on the government's advisory council, there was no doubt who was really in charge. As the Great Asian Propaganda Society, controlled by the army, pointed out, the real reason for the invasion and occupation of Manchuria was to "serve the allied and friendly Japan in her struggle against the Anglo-Saxon world as well as against Comintern aggression".

Nineteen thirty-two saw a wave of political assassinations in Japan. First a former finance minister and then a leading businessman were murdered by right-wing extremists from the poverty-stricken farming community. When one of the assassins was arrested, he told the police his reasons for murder:

It's June when the rice planting starts. But there is not a single grain of rice in the barns. All the warehouses are empty. How can we farmers survive? We cannot afford to buy fertilizers. We have to borrow money from loan sharks who demand such high interest. And when we pay off the interest and the cost of the fertilizers and the tax ... there are nothing but painful calluses left for us. In Japan, those who work so hard to grow the rice cannot afford to eat it. Japan is becoming an unworthy country in which to live ... So I was determined to devote myself to revolution in order to get a better life for those at the bottom of society.

LEFT TO RIGHT: KITAGAWA, TAKEJI AND SAKUE.

 ALL THREE BLEW THEMSELVES UP IN A SUICIDE ATTACK ON CHINESE FORCES DURING THE SHANGHAI INCIDENT.

Extremism was becoming a way of life for many among the poorer elements in Japanese society. In May 1932, there was another coup attempt, this time by nine young officers from the army and navy who broke into the prime minister's house and shot him dead. They then surrendered themselves to the police, safe in the knowledge that they would be leniently treated. The Minister of War, General Araki, was quoted in the papers as saying, "When I consider why these naive youths acted as they did, I cannot hold back my tears. What they did, they did in the genuine belief that it would be good for the empire." All the plotters received light prison sentences that were later commuted without public criticism. Over the next few years similar plots would come thick and fast, some even implicated the emperor's younger brother Prince Chichibu.

The final act in the Mukden Incident came when the League of Nations' Lytton Commission presented its report in the

LEFT: TROOPS CAPTURE THE PAOSHAN GATE IN SHANGHAI, 1937. BELOW: SIGNING OF THE AGREEMENT THAT ESTABLISHED THE 'INDEPENDENT' STATE OF MANCHUKUO, 1932.

M
A
N
C
H
U
K
U
O

autumn of 1932. It condemned the Japanese invasion of Manchuria but concluded that Japan had special rights and privileges in the province. Even this mild and even-handed criticism enraged the ultra-nationalists and instead the Kwantung army invaded the Chinese province of Jehol in January 1933. The League of Nations then adopted the findings of the Lytton Report in full. Japan's chief delegate, Yosuke Matsuoka, who in 1945 would be arrested as a war criminal, made a series of passionate speeches in Japan's defence.

> Japan created the nation of Manchuria, which was essential to maintain the peace in the Orient ... Currently, no one sees the significance of it, but in 30 or 50 years, the world will recognize that Japan was right ... Japan is about to be put on a cross like Christ, and just like he was redeemed ... Japan will be redeemed someday ... We are prepared to be crucified, but we do believe, and firmly believe, that in a very few years world opinion will be changed, and that we also shall be understood by the world as Jesus of Nazareth was.

He then went on to add in words very similar to Hitler's speeches on *Lebensraum* (living space) how "we feel suffocated as we observe internal and external situations. What we are seeking is that which is minimal for living beings. In other words, we are seeking to live. We are seeking room that will let us breathe." Japan then walked out of the league, never to return.

Over the next couple of years, the Japanese continued to consolidate their position in China. The Kwantung army seized the passes through the Great Wall and sought to extend Japanese influence into Inner Mongolia. These conquests were integrated into the Japanese empire with better rail links and communication.

In 1934 Manchukuo was given a new leader in the form of Pu-yi, the last Manchu Emperor of China, but only Hitler's Germany, Mussolini's Italy, a few right-wing Latin American regimes and the Vatican officially recognized its existence. For everyone else the reality of Japanese exploitation was all too obvious. One American observer nicknamed it 'Japankuo'.

# Chapter 8

# THE MARCH TO MILITARISM

ON THE INTERNATIONAL STAGE, JAPAN CONTINUED ITS WITHDRAWAL FROM WHAT IT REGARDED AS RESTRICTIVE INTERNATIONAL AGREEMENTS WITH THE ANNOUNCEMENT THAT IN 1936 IT WOULD ABROGATE THE WASHINGTON AND LONDON AGREEMENTS CONCERNING LIMITATIONS ON NAVAL FORCES. IN FACT, JAPAN HAD ALREADY SECRETLY DESIGNED AND BUILT 18.1-INCH NAVAL GUNS, THE BIGGEST IN THE WORLD BY FAR AT THAT TIME. THEY WERE TO BE MOUNTED IN TWO HUGE NEW BATTLESHIPS, THE *YAMATO* AND THE *MUSASHI*, AGAIN THE LARGEST IN THE WORLD AT OVER 72,000 TONS EACH. OVER THE LAST FIVE YEARS, JAPAN HAD BEEN STEADILY INCREASING ITS MILITARY EXPENDITURE – TO 43.7% OF THE NATION'S BUDGET IN 1934–35, UP FROM 28% IN 1930–31.

The biggest perceived threat at this stage was communist Russia, primarily because of its support for the Chinese communists. For the moment, relations with Britain, the United States and the other Western nations remained strained but neither side was prepared to break the peace. In 1932, one of Japan's elder statesmen, Viscount Kentaro Kaneko, who had helped to write the Meiji constitution, had described Japan's future foreign policy aims in a key speech to a group of senior army officers. It amounted to a Japanese Monroe Doctrine, a plan for the emperor to lead Asia into a new era at the head of a vast new Japanese empire. He had advocated an Asia for the Asians but with the Japanese in charge of course. The idea was quickly picked up by the Japanese press and popularized throughout Japan. The *Japan Times* claimed that "America's control of the destiny of Panama is no more essential to the safety of the United States than is Japan's control of Manchuria to the safety of her empire." Ironically, Kaneko later claimed it was an idea given to him by US President Theodore Roosevelt.

Public criticism of the status quo was now becoming more and more difficult in Japan. There were also increasing limits on academic freedoms. In 1935, one leading legal academic and member of the House of Peers, Professor Tatsukichi Minobe, fell foul of the ultra-nationalists. His crime was that in a series of otherwise conservative books on the Japanese constitution, he had dared to describe the emperor as an "organ" of government. This description was condemned as the "traitorous thoughts of an academic rebel". In the witch-

hunt that followed, Minobe was made to resign all his official posts and his books were banned, all part of a nationwide campaign to "clarify" thinking and teaching on the Japanese state, its divine nature and the purity of its people. Ultra-nationalists later publicly burnt Minobe's books and demanded that he do the only honourable thing and kill himself. Minobe had to withdraw from public life and hide. Later he was wounded in an assassination attempt and his assailant hailed as a hero. Throughout, the government did nothing; in fact they joined in the condemnation.

Militarism and fanatical nationalism were now embedded in Japanese life. One of the most popular songs of the day, "Song of Young Japan", had lyrics written by a naval lieutenant describing Japan's political leaders as being "swollen with pride", and the rich flaunting their wealth and caring nothing for the welfare of Japan. It sang of "brave warriors united in justice ... a million ready like the myriad cherry blossoms to scatter" and a day when "our swords will gleam with the blood of purification". Its simple message was that the military would provide Japan's road to salvation not democracy. War was the answer, not peace. As General Araki said in 1933, "The imperial army's spirit lies in exalting the imperial way and spreading the national virtue. Every single bullet must be charged with the imperial way and the end of every bayonet must have the national virtue burnt into it. If there are those who oppose the imperial way or the national virtue, we shall give them an injection with this bullet and this bayonet."

In 1935, elections were called by the new prime minister, Keisuke Okada, and some of the small left-wing parties and the larger of the moderate groups, the Democratic Party, gained seats in Japan's House of Representatives at the expense of the right-wing. But rather than a sign of a return to sanity this was more likely the result of right-wingers being so alienated from the political system, they had simply declined to vote. In any case, it had little effect as Japan's elected politicians now had little influence or will to resist. Few of the new members of the House of Representatives dared to oppose the military men dominating the cabinet. What was left of parliamentary government in Japan was about to be swept away in a final coup.

ABOVE: THE JAPANESE CRUISER *SENDAI* SHELLS CHINESE POSITIONS NEAR SHANGHAI, AUGUST 1937.
OVERLEAF: JAPANESE MARINES ARE GIVEN A BLESSING AT THE YASUKUNI SHRINE IN TOKYO BEFORE GOING OFF TO WAR, C.1930S.

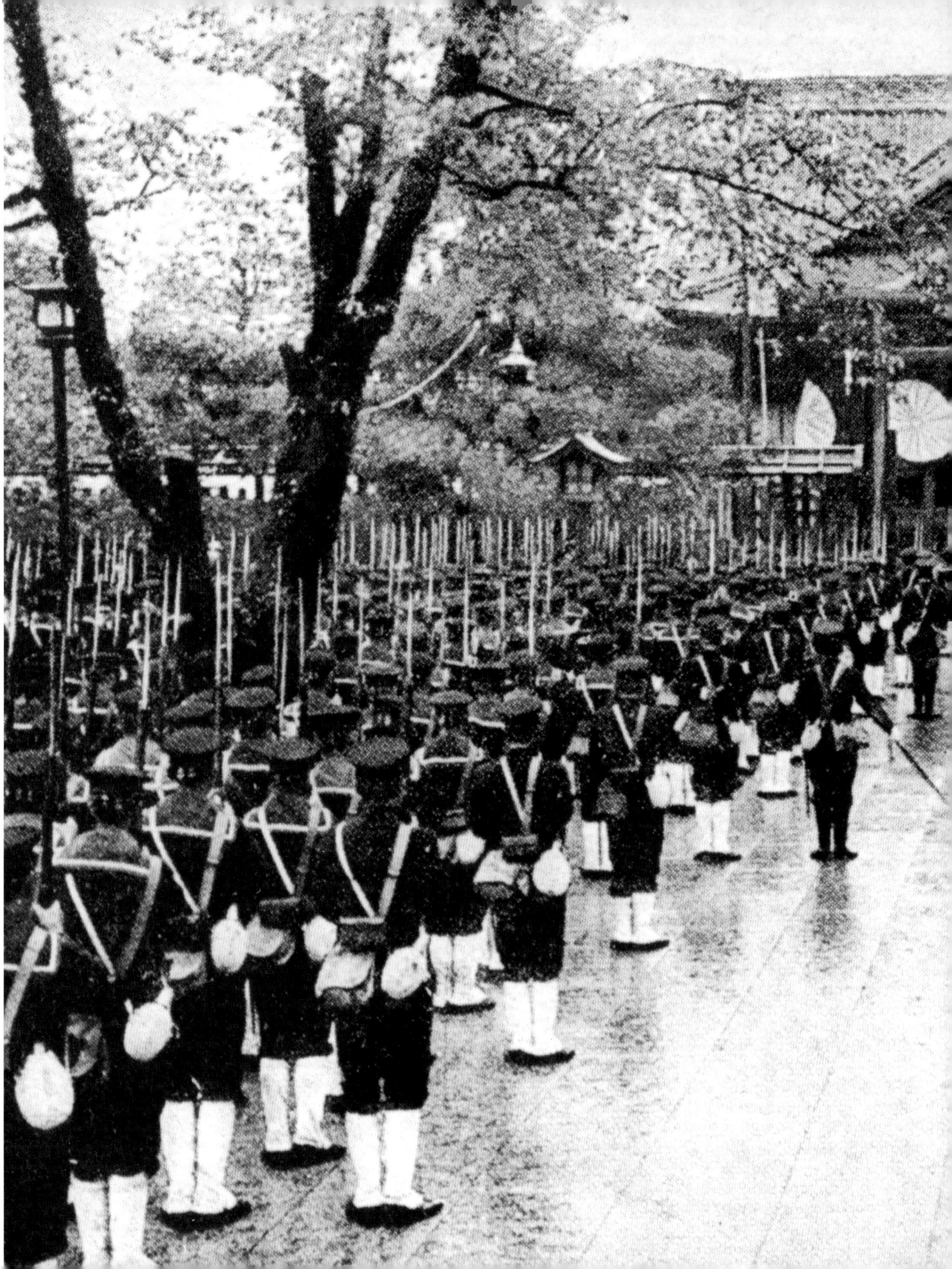

On February 16, 1936, a strange advertisement appeared in the personal columns of the newspaper *Asahi Shimbun*. It read: "Current issues stabilized: there has been a crystallization of the correct judgement of you who are wise and can see into the meaning of things. Let us make every effort, all of us unitedly, to strengthen our national power and to make progress for the empire by leaps and bounds. Leader of the Orient, Marunouchi Art Club, Half-Piercing Solid Star." It was a coded message for a group of rebel army officers to take up arms. Ten days later, in the early morning, 1,500 officers and men of the Imperial Guards Division assembled in their barracks, armed with rifles and machine guns. There had been rumours of a plot flying around Tokyo for months and the rebel leaders had decided to act as they feared they might be transferred to Manchuria.

Manning armoured cars and tanks, some rebels secured key buildings while others were sent on the usual round of political assassinations. Three top politicians were murdered; four others managed to escape, one by hiding in a garden shed. The rebels' motto, emblazoned on their flags was "Revere the emperor! Destroy the traitors!" Their first serious setback came when they were unable to take control of the imperial palace and the emperor himself. Hirohito summoned the minister of war who angered him by simply reading out the rebels' demands, as he had promised them he would do. The emperor then ordered his family, including Prince Chichibu, who had close links with several of the coup leaders, to join him at the palace. He demanded that they do nothing to help the rebels and got them to sign a personal pledge of loyalty.

After three days of stand-off, Hirohito himself brought about a resolution by threatening to lead his own Imperial Guards against the rebels. This was too much for the government, who called on the navy and other loyal forces to intervene. The rebels were then forced to surrender and several of their leaders committed suicide. This time those captured were properly tried, albeit in secret, and many were executed or given long prison sentences. On the surface, it looked as if the failure of the revolt had been a complete success for civil government, but in fact it had simply eliminated one faction, largely made up of hot-headed younger officers who had dreamt of a spiritual rebirth and of restoring a pre-industrial and non-Westernized Japan. A rival faction now came to dominate the military, consisting of older and more sober men who saw that industrialization was needed to make the military strong – leaders who were willing to work with government bureaucrats and top industrialists. Among them was General Hideki Tojo, destined to become Japan's wartime prime minister.

Following the end of the February 1936 coup, the government that had done so little to counter it was forced to resign, and an administration headed by Koki Hirota, a known nationalist, took over. The army immediately blacklisted liberals and moderates in the new cabinet. Hirota had no choice but to agree to the army's candidates and the military takeover was complete, far more cleanly and efficiently than any coup.

Emperor Hirohito had shown uncharacteristic decisiveness during the coup and had done much to bolster the government reaction. But he now returned to a quieter, less interventionist existence. Hirohito spent much time on biological studies of fish, something he enjoyed far more than dealing with politics and the military. Some army leaders found the emperor's hobby peculiar and he was persuaded to keep it a secret. After his efforts to quell the coup, never again would the emperor take such a bold political initiative until Japan's final surrender to the Allies in August 1945.

A FORMAL PORTRAIT OF EMPEROR HIROHITO WITH MOUNT FUJI IN THE BACKGROUND, C. LATE 1920s.

## HIROHITO

The Japanese refer to him posthumously as the Showa Emperor, but during the war he was known as Hirohito. Although in the later years of his life he was seen as a frail old man who ate bacon and eggs every morning and wore a Mickey Mouse watch, it is easy to forget that until 1945, the Emperor of Japan was officially considered to be divine, the Son of Heaven. As a result his subjects were forbidden to look him in the face or even to address him by name.

During and after the war there was debate among the Allies as to what should be done with Hirohito. Should he be indicted as a war criminal along with Prime Minister Tojo for the many atrocities committed in his name by Japanese soldiers throughout Asia and the Pacific? Should he be brought to book for sharing the responsibility for Japan's decision to go to war against the Allies in 1941? To what extent was he aware of the awful things done by his soldiers in Nanjing, by the infamous biological and chemical warfare Unit 731 and the brutality meted out to Allied POWs?

Although it later became clear that Hirohito was completely aware of all of these things and played a full part in the decisions of his various governments, it was decided, largely by General MacArthur in his role as head of the occupying forces in post-surrender Japan, that Hirohito should be spared. It was thought necessary for the recovery of the Japanese nation to maintain continuity in the form of the emperor to prevent the dissolution of Japanese civil society and a possible descent into communism. Once the decision had been made, everyone involved in the war crimes trials was ordered to avoid any mention of Hirohito. Even the defendants played along, despite the fact that it would have helped their cases to claim that they were simply following higher orders. When Tojo told his lawyer that "the subjects of Japan can never say or do anything against His Majesty's will" he was persuaded by the prosecutors not to repeat it in court.

The only real concession to the new reality in Japan was when on January 1, 1946, Hirohito let it be known that he no longer wanted to be thought of as divine. Nevertheless many of his subjects still continued to treat him as if he were a god, bowing in his presence and fiercely protecting his memory.

Officially, Hirohito was the 124th Japanese emperor to sit on the Chrysanthemum Throne and, to date, his reign is the longest of all the emperors. He "ruled" Japan from 1921, when he became regent for his failing father, until his own death in 1989. When he formally gained the Chrysanthemum Throne in 1926, he was given the official title of Showa (Enlightened Peace), highly ironic as his reign turned out.

He was born on April 29, 1901, eldest son of the Emperor Taisho, who was in turn the eldest son of the Emperor Meiji, in whose shadow Hirohito always walked. As a child of seven, Hirohito was enrolled in the Peers' School run by distinguished generals, admirals and academics hand-picked by the highly conservative imperial advisers. From an early age, Hirohito was imbued with the notion of his own divinity, reinforced by a constant round of Shinto ritual and court tradition.

In 1921 Hirohito travelled to Europe, the first time ever for an heir to the throne. It made a huge impression on him, away from the confines of imperial life, particularly the time he spent with the British royal family. He later told his brother, "I discovered freedom for the first time in England." Back in Japan, he became regent for his mentally ill father. Soon after the terrible Kanto earthquake of 1923, a young dissident tried to assassinate Hirohito. He came through the attack unharmed but the outrage caused the resignation of the entire government. In 1924, despite opposition from some imperial advisers, he married Princess Nagako.

PRINCE HIROHITO ON A VISIT TO THE UK IN 1921 MEETS THE PRIME MINISTER DAVID LLOYD GEORGE.

PRINCE HIROHITO WATCHES THE RAF DURING HIS UK VISIT IN 1921.

Two years later, on his father's death, he became emperor amid elaborate ritual and ceremony.

On at least two occasions he attempted to assert his authority with some success. In 1928, when the Japanese prime minister refused to take action against rebellious army officers, Hirohito forced his resignation. The second time was during the failed coup of February 1936.

The next year Japan invaded China and four years later attacked the US fleet at Pearl Harbor. Japan's war only ended when Hirohito agreed to surrender. He announced his decision in a recorded speech played on the radio. It was the first time he had addressed his people publicly and for almost all of them it was the first time they had ever heard his voice. Interestingly, in his speech he never once mentioned surrender or that Japan had lost the war, only that the world situation had changed so dramatically that he was calling on his people to "endure the unendurable". Hearing "the voice of the crane" (as Emperors were known) for the first time caused many of his subjects to break down and weep.

One of the most memorable post-war images of Japan is of Hirohito standing alone on a wooden platform in front of a vast crowd of people in Hiroshima. As he lifts his crumpled grey hat rather hesitantly to acknowledge the people, there is a deafening roar of "Banzai! Banzai! Banzai!" (May you live ten thousand years!) It was a sign that despite the humiliation of defeat, the emperor still embodied the soul of Japan.

Hirohito died on January 7, 1989, after months of a wasting illness, each operation or injection reported in the minute-by-minute detail that Japan's media devotes to baseball averages, weather reports and trade statistics. Although he had presided over the only – and completely catastrophic – total defeat and foreign occupation in Japan's long history, he had also seen it rise phoenix-like from the ashes to become the world's second economic power. Hirohito's Japan of the 1980s dominated the world economically far more effectively than it ever did at the height of its military conquests.

By the mid-1930s, economic recovery was well under way in Japan and full employment had returned. The fighting in China and increased arms production had stimulated the economy and put money back in people's pockets. The Japanese had been taught a dangerous lesson: war was good. Unlike Europeans they had not been through the misery and carnage of the First World War and for the time being could only see the benefits of conflict.

Japan's military was already preparing for the possibility of a world war. Strategic materials, especially iron and oil, were available through trade with the Western powers, but Japan's strategic thinkers realized that Japan could not count on these sources, particularly in wartime. In any conflict with the West, Japan had to prepare for the possibility of a war of long duration and so would need to be self-sufficient in essential commodities.

Through all the chaos and killing of the coups, the Japanese people were still inclined to support the military in its actions abroad, which they saw as being in the best interests of the nation. In 1937, Japanese politics entered another turbulent period. Prime Minister Hirota was forced to resign and his successor lasted only a few months before he too fell. Finally, in June 1937, a new government was formed by Prince Fumimaro Konoye, popular with both the army and the parliament and with the avowed aim of uniting the interests of the military and the rest of the nation.

The outgoing prime minister, Hirota, summed up the mood in Japan when he said, "The military are like an untamed horse left to run wild. If you try head on to stop it, you'll get kicked to death. The only hope is to jump on from the side and try to get it under control while still allowing its head to a certain extent." Hirota had failed to restrain it and the future now looked bleak for any control on the army's influence over civilian affairs. The militarists continued to tighten their grip on power with more and more repressive measures. The Kempeitai (military police) were authorized to tap more phones and intercept more letters. There were more controls on "subversive" literature and liberal politicians now lived in constant fear of assassination. War fever was in the air and Tokyo was full of rumours that the Japanese Army in China was again up to something.

JAPANESE SOLDIERS BIVOUAC FOR THE NIGHT IN CHINA, c.1930s.

# HOLY WAR

# Chapter 4

)T IS NOT ABSOLUTELY CLEAR WHO FIRED THE FIRST SHOT, BUT WHATEVER THE TRUTH OF THE MATTER, A SMALL INCIDENT BETWEEN CHINESE AND JAPANESE SOLDIERS ON THE MARCO POLO BRIDGE OUTSIDE PEKING ON JULY 7, 1937, QUICKLY ESCALATED INTO ALL-OUT WAR. THERE WERE INITIAL ATTEMPTS BY COOLER HEADS ON BOTH SIDES TO DEFUSE THE SITUATION, BUT ONCE AGAIN JAPANESE MILITARISTS SAW IT AS AN OPPORTUNITY TO EXTEND THEIR CONTROL OF CHINA. THERE HAD BEEN REPORTS FROM JAPAN'S INTELLIGENCE NETWORK THAT CHINESE WARLORDS WERE UNITING TO OUST THE JAPANESE INVADERS AND THAT THEY INTENDED TO ATTACK MANCHUKUO. ANTI-CHINESE PROPAGANDA AND A WAVE OF PATRIOTIC FERVOUR SWEPT JAPAN. THE NEWSPAPERS MADE A SENSATION OF THE GOVERNMENT'S DECISION TO SEND REINFORCEMENTS TO CHINA, CLAIMING THAT THE CHINESE WERE NOT TO BE TRUSTED AND THAT ANY AGREEMENTS HAD TO BE BACKED BY FORCE. RESERVISTS AND RECRUITS WERE GIVEN ENTHUSIASTIC SEND-OFFS ALL OVER JAPAN. WHOLE VILLAGES WOULD TURN OUT AND DECK THE LOCAL TRAIN STATION IN FLAGS AND BANNERS; THOSE LEAVING FOR THE FRONT WOULD BE PARADED THROUGH THE STREETS TO THE SHOUTS OF "BANZAI! BANZAI! BANZAI!" BY THE END OF THE MONTH, THREE FULL INFANTRY DIVISIONS WERE ON THEIR WAY TO CHINA.

Characteristically the Japanese never officially declared war and referred to it as "The China Incident". It was left to the Chinese nationalist leader Chiang Kai-shek in a broadcast to his troops on July 31 to announce that the "hope for peace has been shattered" and that China had to fight "to the bitter end". The Chinese nationalists preferred to avoid a formal declaration of war, so Britain and the United States would not have to break their neutrality when supplying arms. The Japanese prime minister simply announced that Japan must now seek a "new order" in Asia; by which he meant a Japanese-led one. War minister General Sugiyama promised the emperor that the war would be over in a month and the nation rejoiced. In fact, the war in China was to last more than eight years. Estimates of Chinese casualties both civilian and military range between ten and twenty million killed with Japanese military deaths in the range of 500,000–750,000. It was anything but clean and quick.

JAPANESE SOLDIERS LAND AT WOOSUNG, OUTSIDE SHANGHAI, AUGUST 1937.

## UNIT 731

In 1936, in the far north-eastern corner of China approximately 20 miles outside the city of Harbin at the village of Ping Fan, the Japanese set up a secret unit that would carry out some of the most gruesome atrocities of the Second World War, comparable to the worst excesses of the Nazis in occupied Europe. It was known simply as Unit 731 and was dedicated to the development and testing of chemical and biological weapons.

Over a six-square-kilometre area, Unit 731 and its sub-units conducted experiments on live human beings involving the use of plague, anthrax and other deadly diseases and the testing of the effects of extreme cold and high air pressure. At least 3,000 people, almost certainly many more, the majority Chinese but also including Russians, Mongolians, Koreans and some Allied POWs, were murdered in this camp. Their remains were then cremated and buried secretly. In addition, maybe as many as 200,000 Chinese died when weapons produced by Unit 731 were tested on the local population and when plague-carrying rats escaped at the end of the war after the camp was destroyed by the retreating Japanese. There were many other similar chemical and biological warfare units established all over China and east Asia: in Hailar, Sun Yang, Beijing, Nanjing, Shanghai, ChangChun, Guangzhou, Singapore, Rangoon, Bangkok and Manila.

Since the end of the war in 1945, sites all over China where the retreating Japanese secretly dumped their stocks of chemical weapons have come to light. For years artillery shells and gas canisters lay hidden and rusting and only gradually began to leak, affecting crops and water systems. As the cases of human poisoning increased, the Chinese authorities began to investigate and the weapons dumps were discovered. After a long and bitter debate, Japan finally agreed to pay for the removal of the chemicals. This desperately needed clean-up is not expected to be completed until 2007 at the very earliest.

It is extremely difficult to uncover the exact extent to which chemical weapons were used by the Japanese army in China as so much of the evidence was deliberately destroyed or hidden at the end of the war. For example, it has only recently been revealed that the Japanese had a massive chemical weapons plant on the island of Okuno Shima near Hiroshima. It was built in 1929 and at its height had over 6,000 workers but never appeared on any maps. One Japanese researcher, Professor Keiichi Tsuneishi, has uncovered army documents showing that over five million poison gas shells and grenades had been produced by the Japanese by 1945.

A former medic with a section of Unit 731 based in Nanjing testified in 1995 that Chinese prisoners were held naked in one-metre-square wire cages. They were then injected with various bacteriological agents over several months. Their reactions were studied and noted and then they were killed at the end of the 'experiment'. A former military policeman admitted sending four arrested Chinese to the unit where they were later killed. He also admitted that this was normal practice for a large number of those arrested by the police. He alone could recall almost 600 Chinese prisoners being sent to Unit 731.

Japan's chemical and biological weapons programme was born in the 1930s by Japanese government scientists who had been alerted to their potential value by the international ban on their use contained in the Geneva Protocol of 1925. Their argument went that if such weapons were so awful that they had to be banned under international law, they must be highly effective and must be investigated at all costs and under the greatest secrecy. The unit was originally set up by General Shiro Ishii in 1936 ostensibly as a water purification plant.

The stories of what took place at Unit 731 make gruesome reading: a European cut into two and preserved in a huge glass jar full of formaldehyde; a Russian mother and daughter put in a gas chamber to die slowly while doctors recorded their last moments; a Chinese peasant infected with plague cut open on an operating table, without anaesthetic, to study the effects of the disease on his internal organs. The victims were known by the members of Unit 731 as *maruta* (logs), a sign of how de-humanized the unit's scientists had become.

Apart from conducting experiments, the unit also carried out field trials of the weapons they were developing. Remote villages around Congshan in northern China were used for one of these trials. In August 1936, Japanese planes circled low and started spraying what looked like smoke over the bemused villagers. Two weeks later the first symptoms appeared and over the next two months 392 people out of a population of 1,200 died from fever and symptoms similar to those of the Black Death that had ravaged Europe in the Middle Ages. At its height, this plague was killing 20 Chinese civilians a day and all of them died excruciating deaths. In November 1942, the Japanese troops moved in to burn down the plague-infected houses and cover up their dirty work. There are still a handful of Chinese peasants who can recall that terrible autumn and they are determined to keep the memory of Japan's dark deeds alive. They have built a small memorial in the village and have renamed a local hill "The Mountain of Remembering Our Hatred".

Evidence has also now come to light that the Japanese military hoped to use chemical and biological weapons against the Allies in the Pacific. In 1944, after the fall of Saipan in the Marianas, Imperial Headquarters in Tokyo came up with a bizarre scheme to hit back at the United States. They planned to launch thousands of large balloons with bombs hanging beneath them that would be carried by the prevailing winds across the Pacific to the US. In the end only 200 balloons made the journey successfully and landed in the US, killing a total of six people in Montana and Oregon. Although these balloons only carried small conventional bombs, there were also plans to load others with biological weapons in an effort to start epidemics of plague or anthrax in the United States. In addition, there was an even more chilling plan, code-named "Cherry Blossoms at Night", to crash planes loaded with the plague into cities in California. The war ended before these particular plans could be put into operation.

One of the main reasons the existence of Unit 731 remained secret for so long was that at the end of the war the Americans agreed to grant its commanders and research scientists immunity from justice in return for the information they had gathered. It was decided that their skills and knowledge would be useful in the expected future struggle with the Soviet Union. So no former member of Unit 731 was ever tried for his crimes and indeed many went on to occupy prominent positions in post-war Japan, as leading scientists, doctors and politicians. General Shiro Ishii was permitted to live peacefully until his death from throat cancer in 1959. There is also much evidence to suggest that Emperor Hirohito was fully aware of the unit's existence. His younger brother Prince Mikasa toured Unit 731's headquarters in China and wrote in his memoirs how gas warfare experiments were carried out on the Chinese.

Apart from Unit 731, atrocities were committed all over China and at all levels of the military. Japanese doctors have come forward to admit to the use of live Chinese patients in the training of army surgeons. Chinese prisoners would be routinely used to practise techniques of amputation and field surgery, and when the tests were over, they were simply killed.

The Japanese government has never formally apologized for Unit 731's activities, nor has it even fully acknowledged its existence, despite overwhelming evidence. Only in August 1997 did the Supreme Court in Tokyo rule that "academics" now accepted its existence. Even by Japanese standards this was a most begrudging and belated admission. There is no doubt the war in China was an extremely brutal one involving widespread atrocities, and it has left a deep and bitter legacy in both China and Japan.

With Japan's campaign in China gathering pace, international criticism grew. President Roosevelt, in a famous speech in Chicago in October 1937, described how "Without a declaration of war and without warning or justification of any kind, civilians, including vast numbers of women and children, are being ruthlessly murdered with bombs from the air... Innocent peoples, innocent nations are being cruelly sacrificed to a greed for power and supremacy which is devoid of all sense of justice and humane considerations ... " He went on to describe such a war as an "epidemic" that needed to be "quarantined" if it was not to spread to the rest of the world. Although he did not mention Japan by name, the speech was seen by many as a direct attack on Japanese policy in Asia and a call for concerted international action. However, Roosevelt found little support in the US or among his international allies for any intervention and the Japanese response was to refer back to America's own history of expansion. Yosuke Matsuoka, the diplomat who had led Japan out of the League of Nations, wrote: "What country in its expansion era has ever failed to be trying to its neighbours? Ask the American Indian or the Mexican how excruciatingly trying the young United States used to be once upon a time." The Western world had expanded through military conquest so why shouldn't Japan? But the Japanese were still not ready to take things a stage further and openly confront another major power so when their planes sank a US gunboat on the Yangtze River later in the year, they issued a complete apology.

TYPE 92 LIGHT TANK, USED FOR SCOUTING IN CHINA, 1930S.

愛國27(報電三列)

寶山縣學堂

JAPANESE SOLDIERS CAPTURE PAOSHAN GATE IN SHANGHAI, AUGUST 1937.

The Japanese advances in China were at first swift and hundreds of towns and cities fell with relative ease. There were genuine hopes of it all being over quickly. On July 30, the Japanese captured the strategic city of Tientsin, with its international settlement, and set a pattern for future conduct when it was looted and burned, a tactic designed to show the Chinese that resistance was futile.

There was little comparison between the two armies. Japan had 17 divisions in China, almost 400,000 men, equipped with tanks, artillery and aircraft. They were well trained and properly supplied with ammunition and supplies; and Japan's highly efficient army reserve could swiftly replace any battlefield casualties. The Chinese army was made up of almost two million soldiers in 191 divisions spread over the entire country. The great majority were poorly trained, poorly equipped and poorly motivated. Chinese soldiers had often been enlisted at gunpoint and would desert whenever the opportunity arose. Rifles were in short supply and machine guns were even fewer in number. The Chinese had virtually no artillery, tanks or motor transport. In many respects it was a hugely unequal contest, but one which was evened out by China's vastness and the dogged determination of the Chinese to resist the Japanese invaders.

ABOVE: JAPANESE SOLDIERS ADVANCE IN CHINA, 1937.
OVERLEAF: JAPANESE PROPAGANDA POSTER WIDELY USED IN CHINA IN THE 1930s.

Whenever there was a set-piece battle the Chinese were usually outgunned, outmanoeuvred and outfought, but they simply slipped away to fight another day and adopted the highly effective tactic of hit and run. This enraged the Japanese and fostered an atmosphere of barbarous hatred. Both sides were guilty of atrocities but the Japanese were more thorough and ruthless. The Chinese would flood a plain to stop a Japanese advance, while the Japanese would burn down whole villages and kill the inhabitants. One Japanese reporter even described a killing contest between two Japanese lieutenants as they fought their way through China. One of them boasted to his rival: "I think I will have made roughly a hundred dead before we arrive at Nanjing... so I am afraid you have lost the game."

The atrocity that quite rightly attracted most attention and condemnation, and is still a bone of contention today, was the infamous Rape of Nanjing. Chiang Kai-shek, the Chinese nationalist leader, had made it his capital and the fighting to capture it in November and December 1937 was brutal and bloody, but was nothing compared to what occurred once the city finally fell on December 13. Benumbed by years of brutal military training and a propaganda machine that portrayed the Chinese as animals, Japanese soldiers went on a rampage of looting, burning, mutilation, raping and murder. They killed indiscriminately and for no apparent reason other than bloodlust. Men, women, children, old and young, soldier and civilian, all were brutalized and killed. Nor was it over in one brief bloody moment but continued for weeks, the Japanese commanders either unwilling or unable to stop the carnage. The final death toll is hotly contested, ranging from 30,000 to over a quarter of a million. A few Japanese right-wing revisionists even try to deny it happened at all, but the evidence – from diaries of witnesses both Chinese and Western, letters from Japanese soldiers themselves detailing what happened, to photographs and even black and white movie film – is overwhelming. Nanjing ranks alongside the very worst atrocities of the twentieth century. At the time, no details of the carnage were reported in Japan; military censors saw to that. Instead the capture of the city was hailed as a great victory for the Japanese army. Rallies and parades were held all over Japan, schoolchildren waved flags and the nation was encouraged to contribute more to the war effort.

By the end of 1937, the war in China did not look like ending quickly. More troops, more tanks, more planes were sent from Japan. In August, China had signed a military pact with the Soviet Union. For years, the Chinese Communists had been arguing for an all-out war to rid China of the Japanese, and now they joined with the warlords and the Nationalists. The Communists announced their "unswerving loyalty" and "unqualified support" for Generalissimo Chiang Kai-shek. The Chinese Red Army was reorganized and renamed the Eighth Route Army and was assigned to fight under his command.

Attempts to end the war through a negotiated settlement were continually defeated by the reluctance of either side to give ground. In January 1938, frustrated by Chiang Kai-shek's apparent unwillingness to compromise, Prime Minister Konoye made it clear that Japan would no longer deal with his government. Instead they would concentrate all their efforts on annihilating both him and his regime. The China Incident, as it was still known in Japan, had become a 'Holy War' that would last another seven years.

In September 1937, a Campaign for National Spiritual Mobilization had been launched throughout Japan. At first it just issued lots of propaganda and advice on patriotic activities to help the war effort. For example, it published a list of seven "Principles for Daily Living": to rise early, offer gratitude and thanks, cooperate with others for the sake of Japan, do public labour service, observe strict punctuality, be thrifty at all times and maintain strict physical and spiritual discipline. It later became more practical in its advice, helping to coordinate the activities of the thousands of patriotic groups that had sprung up in response to the war in China. By the end of 1940, almost 200,000 community councils had been formed all over Japan. Groups of women would make up "welfare packs" to send to the troops at the front or stand on busy street corners and invite passers-by to sew a stitch on the thousand-stitch belts given to soldiers as good luck charms. Children would collect scrap iron to be melted down for munitions. Farmers would get together to look after the land of those away at the war. The whole country was officially put on a war footing with the passing of the National Mobilization Law in March 1938. From then on the government took control of anything in the name of the war effort.

## SECRET POLICE

One of the most feared organizations in Japan and its overseas empire in the 1930s and 1940s was the Kempeitai (Military Police), whose function was to keep both the Japanese people and the inhabitants of the conquered territories in line with government policy. Any dissent was ruthlessly sought out and eliminated. At the end of the war, many of the lesser war crimes trials involved the activities of former members of the Kempeitai and its allied organizations.

The old samurai police force of the shoguns had been abolished during the Meiji Restoration of the late nineteenth century. Toshiyoshi Kawaji, the Tokyo Metropolitan Police Commissioner, went on a tour of Europe's police forces in 1872 and was most impressed by those of France and Prussia. They became the models for the new Japanese police. This new police force took on a wide range of responsibilities that extended far beyond normal criminal duties and included the control of most areas of Japanese society.

The Kempeitai was set up on January 4, 1881. At first it consisted of only 349 men who were not only to police the military but had some civilian duties as well, especially with regard to the new conscription laws. The Kempeitai was divided into two sections, one for dealing with Dai Nippon Teikoku Kaigun (Imperial Japanese Navy), the other for the Dai Nippon Teikoku Rikugun (Imperial Japanese Army). From the beginning, one of its primary duties was *chian iji* (maintenance of order), a catch-all that came to cover a wide variety of "crimes" and gave its officers carte blanche to root out dissent in any form.

In 1901, the Tokubetsu Koto Keisatsu (Tokko or Special Higher Police) was established. It was a civilian counterpart to the military Kempeitai, targeting any dissent from imperial rule and Japanese expansionism. The Tokko comprised six departments (special police work, foreign surveillance, Koreans in Japan, labour relations, censorship and arbitration) and had overseas offices in Shanghai, London and Berlin. The Tokko investigated a large number of internal matters including Japanese people listening to foreign music or reading foreign books, communists, pacifists and those not showing proper respect to the emperor. A network of informants (*Tonari Gumi* or neighbourhood associations) was established in every building, street and neighbourhood in Japan. By 1936, the Tokko had arrested over 59,000 people. Prisoners were forced to write accounts of how they had become infused with "dangerous thoughts", rewriting these confessions until their interrogators were happy with the results. These were then used to prove their criminal guilt.

Throughout this period, the Kempeitai's powers were continually strengthened through revisions of the infamous Peace Preservation Law. For example, in 1925 the law prohibited the organizing of groups that had as their objective the alteration of the "national polity" (a state headed by an emperor) or those opposing the concept of private property. It led to the mass arrest of Communists, trade union organizers and radicals, and under the new law the minimum time any person convicted spent in prison was six months no matter how trivial their offence. In 1941, another revision extended the law to liberals and intellectuals with no political affiliation and people who held religious beliefs at odds with the state-sponsored Shinto.

In many respects the Kempeitai and the Tokko were similar to Hitler's Gestapo and Stalin's KGB. Their officers were involved in all aspects of law enforcement and social control. They were the regular police force patrolling a city or village, but were also the censors opening the post and checking newspapers. Suspects were considered guilty upon arrest, and torture was regularly used to gain confessions. Some have suggested that the Kempeitai and the Tokko were the most accomplished torturers since the medieval Catholic inquisition. Under the Japanese legal concept of *kikosaku* (severe punishment without martial law involvement) the secret police were investigator, prosecutor, judge, jury and executioner all in one. They helped turn Japan into an efficient and ruthless police state.

# A FAITH IN VICTORY

**B**Y THE LATE 1930S, JAPAN WAS FAST BECOMING A TOTALITARIAN STATE. THERE WERE NEW LAWS TO TIGHTEN PRESS CENSORSHIP, INCREASE GOVERNMENT CONTROL OF PRICES AND WAGES AND END THE RIGHT TO STRIKE. IN OCTOBER 1940, DANCE HALLS WERE CLOSED, DENOUNCED AS FRIVOLOUS AND UNPATRIOTIC. BARS HAD RESTRICTED HOURS AND MANY RESTAURANTS CLOSED DOWN. THERE WAS A STRICT ECONOMY DRIVE WITH THE SLOGAN, "WASTE NOT, WANT NOT UNTIL WE WIN". SHOPS WERE TOLD NOT TO STOCK ANY NON-ESSENTIAL MERCHANDISE, EXPENSIVE COSMETICS WERE BANNED AND WESTERN HAIRSTYLES DISCOURAGED.

Any form of criticism, however mild, was outlawed. All aspects of Japanese life were organized to bring the people and economy to a peak of military efficiency. Prime Minister Konoye had appointed General Araki minister of education and militarism further penetrated the education system. Schoolchildren were taught the Imperial Rescript to Soldiers and Sailors, the nineteenth-century imperial decree that had established a strict code of conduct for Japan's military. School sports days began to resemble army parades as young boys drilled with wooden rifles and put on public displays of the martial art of kendo. Ordinary citizens were encouraged to support the war effort through public donations. By the end of August 1937, ten million yen had been received at the war office and six million yen at the navy office. These were huge sums as the average monthly salary of a government employee at that time was just 75 yen.

As a sign of their patriotic commitment, families that had sent a soldier to the front were allowed to hang a plaque outside their homes that said, "Home of Honour". Later, when the casualties started flooding in (there were 185,000 deaths in China before 1941), families would hang out black flags.

In April 1938, the budget allocation for the Japanese army was doubled, bringing its strength up to 34 divisions. There were now more than 1.5 million Japanese soldiers in China. Two new offensives were launched but still the war dragged on and final victory seemed more distant than ever. Then on July 29 a new front was opened with an attack on the Russians on the Soviet–Manchukuo border near Changkufeng. At first the Japanese were successful, but the Russians poured in reinforcements including a motorized brigade, and launched a counter-offensive on August 6. The Japanese were forced to retreat with over 500 dead and more than 1,000 wounded. Both sides then agreed a ceasefire.

ABOVE: A TYPICAL SMALL FARMING VILLAGE IN JAPAN, C.1940S.
OVERLEAF: TYPE 88 75MM ANTI-AIRCRAFT GUN IN CHINA, 1930S.

In May, in a strange quirk of Japanese politics one of the few army generals who dared to oppose the war in China, Ugaki, became Japan's foreign minister. He had always argued that a war in China would interrupt plans for the expansion of Japan's industrial base and consume costly imports of oil, machine tools and steel. He wanted to end the fighting as soon as possible through a negotiated peace, but by this stage his was a lone and deeply unpopular voice. Frustrated and under pressure, he resigned in September 1938. In October, after months of bombing, the Japanese captured the southern city of Guangzhou, but again the Chinese armies simply melted away to continue their war of attrition.

In November 1938, the Japanese announced their "New Order" for East Asia. A Chinese government headed by Wang Ching-wei, a puppet of the Japanese and a rival to Chiang Kai-shek, was set up in Nanjing. Under this New Order, Chinese trade would concentrate on Japan with nations such as the United States, Britain, Germany and France getting the leftovers. A firm advocate of this policy was the rising General Hideki Tojo, former Chief of Staff of the Kwantung army and now a vice minister of war. General Tojo saw the New Order as a blueprint for cooperation between the Chinese and Japanese, with China contributing raw materials and Japan contributing capital, skills in technology and administration "for the mutual benefit of both countries". At least, this was how he would later justify the war in China to the Allied judges at his war crimes trial after the war.

In 1939, the fighting against the Russians along the Manchukuo border flared again. And again the Japanese were outclassed and beaten, this time decisively. In August a Soviet counter-offensive, with massed tanks and artillery, outflanked the Japanese. Two regiments were surrounded and their commanders committed suicide. Casualties in some units were over 70%. The Japanese lost 18,000 dead and wounded, five times more than the Soviets. Another ceasefire was called and the fighting ended. Perhaps luckily for the Japanese, Stalin was at the time more interested in what was going on in Europe.

SCHOOLCHILDREN IN TOKYO CELEBRATE THE CAPTURE OF NANKING, DECEMBER 1937.

Relations between Nazi Germany and Japan had been developing for some time, although not always through official channels. An Anti-Comintern pact – against Soviet Russia – had been signed with Hitler in 1936, negotiated by the army via its rabidly pro-Nazi military attaché in Berlin, Hiroshi Oshima. The emperor's younger brother Prince Chichibu had also made a visit to Germany in 1937, meeting Hitler, attending the annual Nuremburg rally in September and helping to seal the relationship between the two nations. Although the Nazi–Soviet Pact of 1939 provoked a slight hiccup in the alliance, it was formally sealed with the Tripartite Pact of September 1940, with Italy as the third partner. With a new world war already under way, Japan would fight alongside the Axis powers against the Allies.

While relations with Germany improved, those with Britain and the United States continued to deteriorate. The main issue, as ever, was China, with Britain and the US condemning Japanese expansion. This was partly out of revulsion at the brutality of the Japanese conquest and partly out of concern for the consequences to their own spheres of influence. For their part, the Japanese military command started to plan for war with the old colonial powers in Asia. As German victories mounted, there were growing calls among the militarists in Japan to seize the opportunity. Now was the time to attack while the West was preoccupied with events in Europe. There were dissenting voices. Ironically the most influential was that of Admiral Yamamoto, the man who would later devise the attack on Pearl Harbor. From the start, he had no illusions about the difficulties involved in fighting the Western powers and the United States in particular. His views became so well known that he received death threats from ultra-nationalists, accusing him of being a British and American sympathizer.

The problem for the Japanese government was one of natural resources. The military was now using almost 30,000 gallons of oil a day in China, and it needed iron and steel and rubber to build tanks, guns and ships. Japan had to rely almost completely on imports for these commodities, and most came

THE JAPANESE BATTLESHIP *HYUGA*, LAUNCHED IN 1917 AND SUNK ON JULY 24, 1945 NEAR KURE, JAPAN.

## TOJO

Hideki Tojo was born in Tokyo on December 30, 1884. He joined the army at a young age and his military service included periods in Switzerland and Germany. He was promoted to major general in 1933 and became head of the Kwantung army in September 1935. Raised to lieutenant general, he was chief of staff to the Kwantung army's *Kempeitai* (military police) between March 1937 and May 1938. In May 1938, Tojo was appointed vice-minister of war. However, after just six months he resigned and returned to the armed services. Tojo held extreme right-wing views and was an admirer of Nazi Germany. He was also a vehement anti-communist and feared the long-term plans of Soviet Russia to the extent that in 1938 he supported the idea of pre-emptive air strikes on the Soviet Union.

When Tojo joined the government as war minister in July 1940, to many he was still a relative unknown. To those who did know him he was an obstinate man and a hard worker, totally dedicated to the job in hand. Known as "the Razor" for his ability to cut through work and people, he was no intellectual, but an army man through and through and both highly regarded and feared by his colleagues. He was seen as incorruptible and an absolutely rigid disciplinarian. Unlike many other generals, he was untainted by connection with any of the coups of the 1930s and in fact had acted swiftly in crushing support for them. For him revolt was unthinkable and inexcusable. From the start of his time in government, he advocated an aggressive foreign policy and strongly opposed plans to withdraw Japanese troops from China and Korea.

On October 16, 1941, just two months before Pearl Harbor, Tojo became prime minister of Japan. He initially backed the foreign ministry's efforts to reach an agreement with the United States, but simultaneously developed plans for a surprise attack on the US Pacific fleet. Finally convinced that a negotiated deal was impossible, he ordered the attack on Pearl Harbor on December 7, 1941.

Tojo also held the posts of Minister of War, Home Minister and Foreign Minister. From February 1944 he was also Chief of the General Staff. In mid-1944 he staked his political future on the battle for the Mariana Islands, and when they fell in July, he was forced to resign. At the surrender of Japan in September 1945, Tojo was top of the list of war criminals the Allies wished to prosecute. The charges against him included 36 counts of "crimes against peace"; 16 counts of murder; and three counts of "other conventional war crimes and crimes against humanity". Tojo and his co-defendants were accused of conspiring to wage "aggressive war" between 1928 and 1945 in order to gain "domination and control of East Asia". More specifically, Tojo was also accused of authorizing the use of Allied POWs as slave labour, resulting in many thousands of deaths from maltreatment and malnourishment.

When the American military police arrived to arrest him in September 1945, Tojo tried to commit suicide by shooting himself in the chest, but survived and was made to stand trial. His face came to symbolize the Japanese enemy with his closely shaved head and small round spectacles. He was the most senior Japanese to be executed for war crimes and was hanged on December 23, 1948.

While in prison during his trial he was allowed to write a diary, in which he attempted to justify his actions and those of the Japanese government during the war. It is a prime example of how many Japanese at the time – and revisionist right-wingers ever since – have tried to portray Japan as a victim of the Western colonial powers and to justify its aggression as self-defence.

In answer to why Japan waged war against China (although he always denied this was a war), he wrote:

Immediately before the beginning of the Great East Asian War [the Japanese name for the Second World War in the Pacific] Japan was still engaged in the unfortunate Sino-Japanese War, which had already gone on for more than four years. Throughout that period, Japan had made honest efforts to keep the destruction of war from spreading and, based on the belief that all nations of the world should find their places, had followed a policy designed to restore an expeditious peace between Japan and China. Japan was ensuring the stability of East Asia while contributing to world peace. Nevertheless, China was unfortunately unable to understand Japan's real position, and it is greatly to be regretted that the Sino-Japanese War became one of long duration.

PRIME MINISTER GENERAL HIDEKI TOJO, 1941–44.

from the United States, Britain and the Dutch East Indies. To feed its war machine and maintain its freedom of action, Japan needed to take control of the sources of these materials to the south in British Malaya, French Indochina and the Dutch East Indies.

In June 1940, the Japanese government, prompted by the army, demanded the British close the Burma Road, the Chinese Nationalists' supply lifeline. Fully occupied with the threat of a Nazi invasion, the British agreed. In July 1940, a new government was formed in Tokyo with a far more aggressive cabinet. The new war minister was General Hideki Tojo, a prime supporter of war to further Japan's aims.

Nazi domination of continental Europe was completed with the surrender of France in June 1940. In August, the Japanese government demanded that the Vichy French authorities allow it to use airfields in Indochina to attack the Chinese Nationalists. At a high-level imperial conference on September 19, 1940, Tojo outlined Japan's plans for the future: "We should settle the China incident quickly and at the same time cope with the Southern Question, taking advantage of favourable opportunities. As for the Netherlands East Indies, it is decided that we will try to obtain vital materials by diplomatic means and that we might use force, depending on the circumstances."

When the Japanese moved into parts of Indochina on September 22, Britain reopened the Burma Road and the United States embargoed sales of scrap metal to Japan. Detailed planning now started for a war with the United States. As it would be largely a sea campaign, the navy took the lead. Admiral Yamamoto, now vice-minister of the navy, was convinced that the only hope for success lay in a sudden devastating blow to bring the United States to the negotiating table. After the US Navy moved the base of its Pacific fleet from the American west coast to the "impregnable" Pearl Harbor in May 1940, he began to plan a surprise attack. When he showed an early version to his colleagues, they thought he was mad. Yamamoto ignored them and continued to refine his plans.

The United States had responded to the move into Indochina by ending its commercial treaty with Japan, at a stroke cutting off 70% of its supply of scrap iron and steel. For the moment an even more damaging oil embargo was avoided, but tensions remained high. The US State Department advised all US nationals, except for essential military personnel to leave East Asia. The Nazis, for their part, were doing all they could to encourage Japan to enter the war. They favoured an attack on the naval base of Singapore to increase the pressure on the British Empire but the Japanese refused to be rushed.

Throughout 1941, a series of imperial conferences were held to discuss Japan's future aims. The plans which emerged involved a full-scale occupation of French Indochina, followed by an invasion of British Malaya and then the Dutch East Indies. What was still not clear was the effect this would have on the United States. The first test came when Japan fully invaded Indochina in July. The US immediately reacted with a complete trade embargo, crucially including oil. In the next few days both the British and the Dutch followed suit, completely cutting off Japan's major sources of oil. The Americans, British and Dutch refused to restore the flow unless the Japanese withdrew all their forces from both China and Indochina. War now looked more likely than ever. On September 6, 1941, another conference was held in Tokyo at which it was decided to continue the negotiations with the Americans until October 10. If nothing had changed by then, the decision to go to war would be made.

The Japanese propaganda machine went into overdrive at home and abroad, to explain itself to its own people and to the world outside. The American, British, Chinese and Dutch encirclement – or the ABCD encirclement as it was known – was strangling Japan which was locked in a struggle for survival. Japan had no choice but to go to war. And this would be a "Holy War" that could extend from China to the rest of East Asia.

ADMIRAL YAMAMOTO, THE ARCHITECT OF THE SURPRISE ATTACK ON PEARL HARBOR.

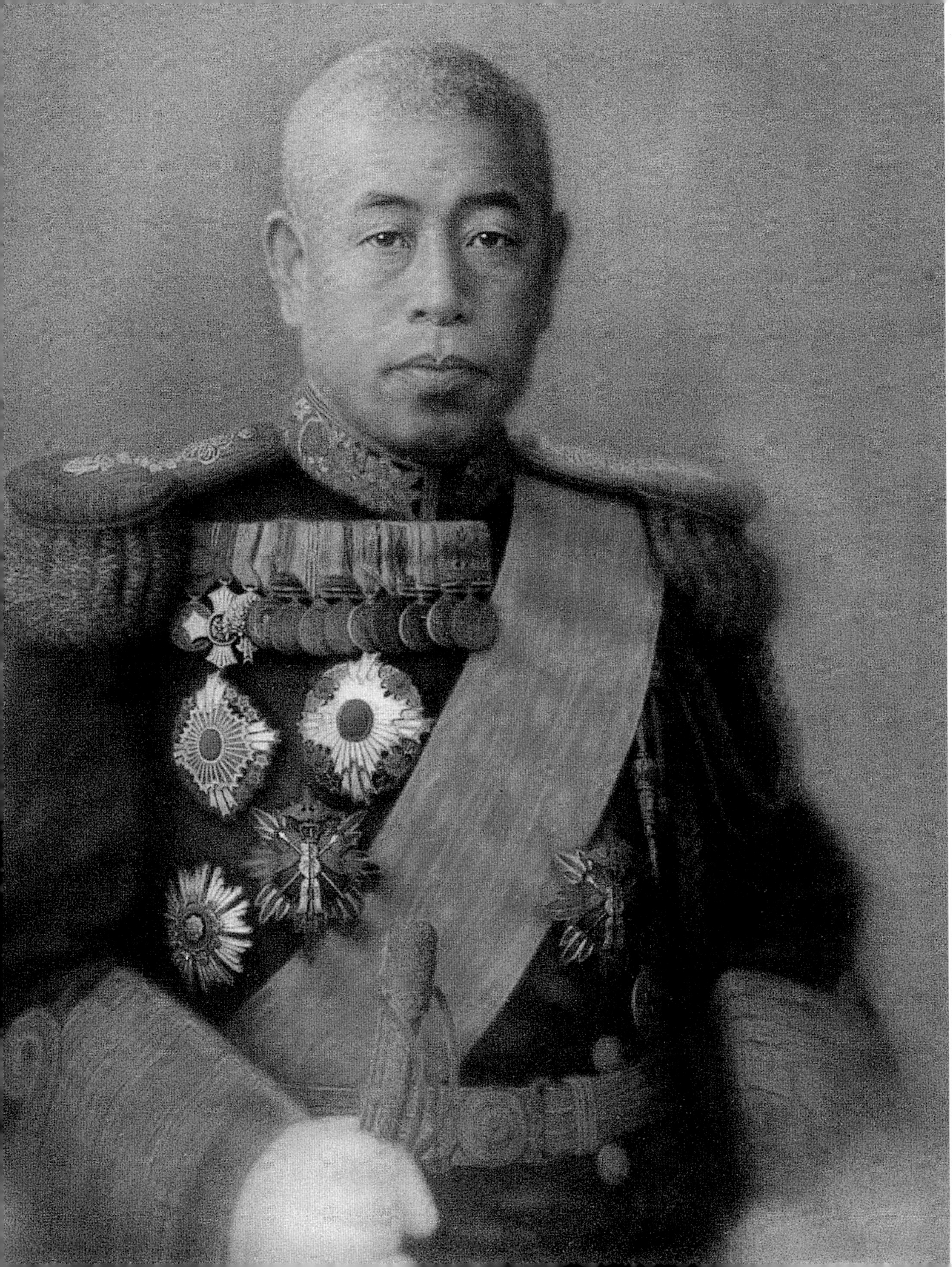

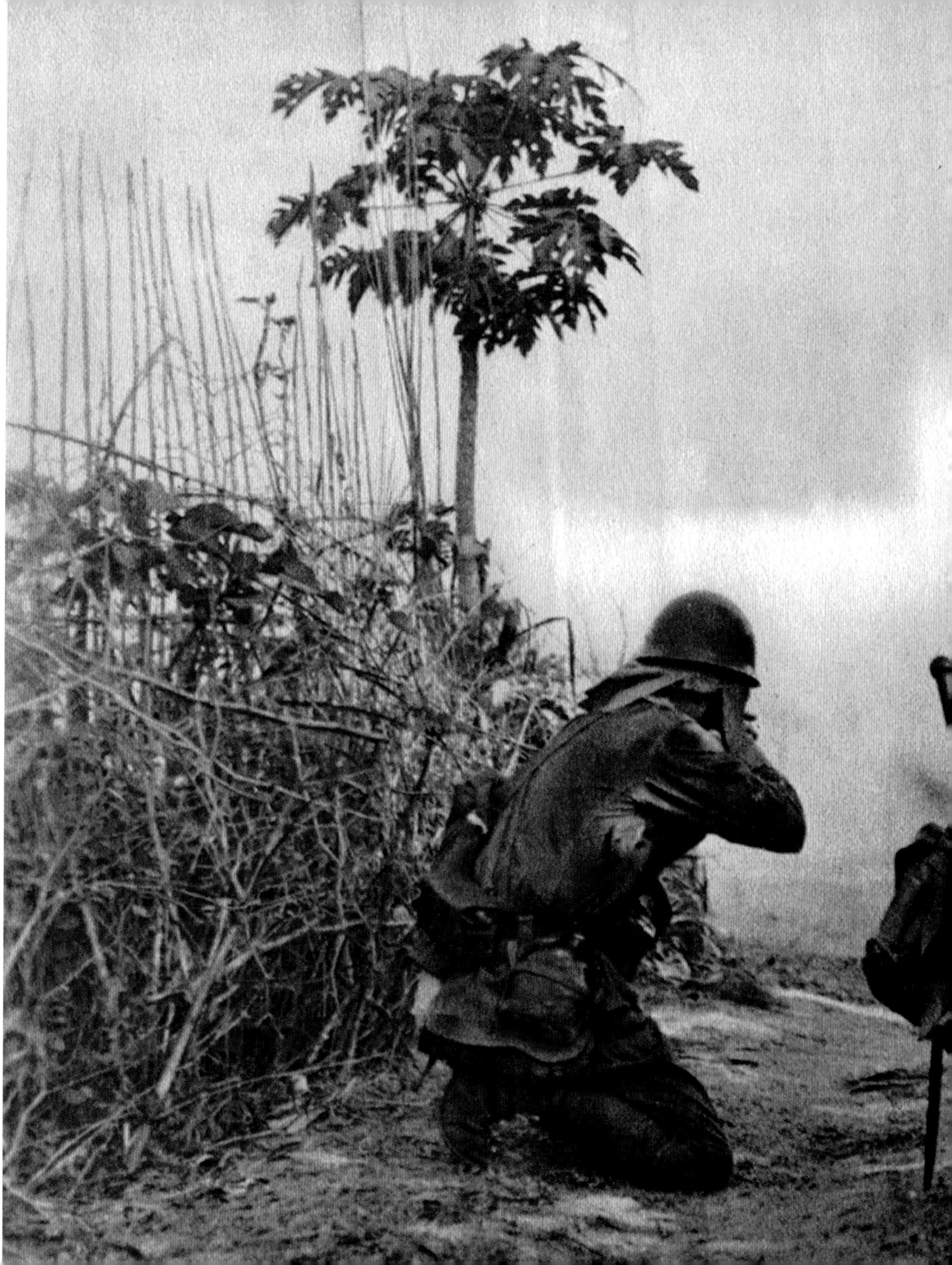

Admiral Yamamoto's plans were now well advanced. A bay near Kagoshima in the south of Japan had been found that closely resembled Pearl Harbor so that detailed training for the attack could begin. Landing troops on Hawaii was rejected, although it would have given the Japanese greater control over the Pacific. The navy was concerned that troop transports would slow down any attacking force and the army complained that it could not spare any soldiers. The planners were receiving regular intelligence updates thanks to a highly effective spy network in Hawaii based in the consulate and run by one of the consular staff, Takeo Yoshikawa.

The Americans had several warnings that an attack on Pearl Harbor was a possibility. Earlier in the year, Peru's ambassador to Japan had overheard something, and had told an American embassy official. The US had also broken Japanese diplomatic codes and was listening in on most of their communications, but still nothing was done. The Americans were more worried about the possibility of sabotage from within rather than an attack from outside. Both in Hawaii and all along the west coast of the USA there were significant populations of Japanese-Americans and they were coming under increasing suspicion.

Elsewhere in the Pacific, American strategists believed that the Japanese were unlikely to attack the Philippines. They were convinced that the American and Filipino forces led by General MacArthur could more than adequately defend themselves. The British and Dutch also felt secure in

HEAVY CRUISER *MOGAMI*, BADLY DAMAGED DURING THE BATTLE OF MIDWAY AND SUNK AT THE BATTLE OF LEYTE GULF, OCTOBER 25, 1944.

their colonial territories. The Japanese were not thought of as good fighters or flyers. Moreover, MacArthur had received reinforcements from the US mainland and Churchill had dispatched two warships to Singapore.

The October deadline for a resolution of negotiations with the Americans came and went and still war was not declared. The pressure became too great for the Japanese government and it resigned. The new prime minister was General Tojo himself. He immediately leaked details of cabinet meetings to better prepare the nation for war. He himself was already convinced that war was the only option. One Tokyo newspaper proclaimed, "The Japanese spokesman in Washington is reported to have warned the United States that if there should not be any development in the Japanese–American negotiations, it will lead to Japan's applications of 'self-defence' measures." This was an obvious euphemism for war. On November 5, another imperial conference set early December as the date for commencing hostilities against the Americans, British and Dutch, with the proviso that an attack could be called off if negotiations with the Americans were successful. On November 18 the Japanese fleet left for a secret rendezvous point in the Kurile Islands and on November 26 it started its voyage south towards Hawaii. Diplomatic negotiations continued right up to the moment of the attack. In part this was a sincere attempt to seek peace and in part a means of stringing the Americans along until it was too late.

On November 27, US Secretary of War Stimson was told of a large Japanese force sailing from Shanghai. General MacArthur in the Philippines was warned that hostilities could break out at any moment but that he should not make the first move. Commanders at Pearl Harbor were ordered to prepare themselves against attempts at sabotage, which meant that all aircraft were moved into the middle of the runways and parked close together for greater security.

On November 28, Roosevelt met with his war cabinet. Stimson suggested a pre-emptive strike against any Japanese force moving southward; others preferred to warn the Japanese that the US would attack once the force crossed a certain line. In Hawaii, the battleships, cruisers and destroyers of the US Pacific fleet lay at anchor but of the three all-important aircraft carriers, one had been sent to Wake Island, another to Midway and the third was in San Diego for repairs. The stage was set for war.

The final pre-war imperial conference was held on December 1. Tojo led the speeches:

> At the moment our Empire stands at the threshold of glory or oblivion. We tremble with fear at the presence of His Majesty. We subjects are keenly aware of the great responsibility we must assume from this point on. Once His Majesty reaches a decision to commence hostilities, we will all strive to repay our obligations to him, bring the government and the military ever closer together, resolve that the nation united will go on to victory, make an all-out effort to achieve our war aims, and set His Majesty's mind at ease.

The next day, Yamamoto was ordered to send the pre-arranged signal to the fleet steaming at full speed towards Hawaii: "Climb Mount Niitake" meant the attack was on and war was now all but unstoppable.

The warnings to the Americans now came thick and fast. It is claimed that the Japanese fleet heading for the Hawaiian Islands broke radio silence for a short time and that this enabled US radio direction finders to locate the attack force. There were also claims that the Dutch knew that the Japanese were going to attack Pearl Harbor and that they passed a report on to the Americans that two Japanese aircraft carriers were moving east halfway between Japan and Hawaii. Information from the breaking of Japanese naval codes also continued to warn of a possible attack but it was sent from Washington to Pearl Harbor by telegram and so did not arrive until the day after the attack. Whatever the truth or otherwise of these warnings, the fact is the Japanese achieved total surprise when they attacked Pearl Harbor.

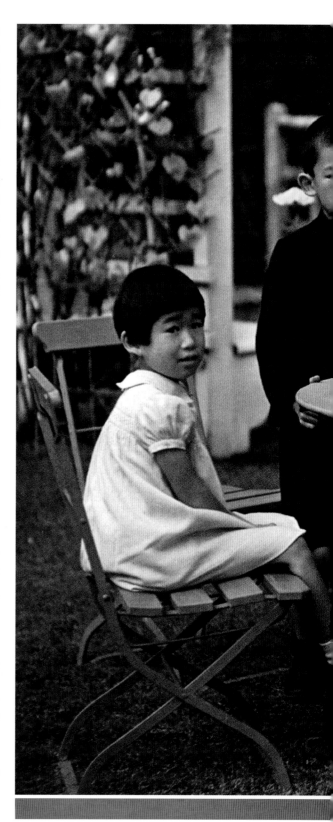

A GROUP OF JAPANESE CHILDREN, C.1940S.

another was filmed by an unnamed cameraman aboard the USS *St Louis*, one of the few big ships that successfully got underway during the raid and made it out to sea; and the last was shot by a naval rating with his personal camera aboard the destroyer USS *Mugford*.

By its very nature – and the fact that it is colour – all this footage is as important and as valuable to the American nation as the infamous Zapruder footage of the assassination of President Kennedy, if not more so as it records the fate of thousands of Americans, not just one. And it was shot by government employees, four sailors and an army sergeant, while on active duty, so that there should be little doubt as to who owns the film – the American nation. But since that day in December 1941, almost none of that colour film has been shown publicly. Despite the best efforts of generations of film archivists and researchers, it has mysteriously disappeared without trace.

In the aftermath of the attack, the US government seized all film shot, official and otherwise, and placed a ban on its use. The argument was that it might reveal the extent of the damage to the enemy. The fact that the Japanese had almost certainly filmed and photographed the attack themselves (which they did) made this argument spurious. What seems a stronger reason is that the raid in all its gory detail was so embarrassing and potentially damaging to American morale that it was best left unseen for the time being. It was also a particularly painful episode for the navy and army commanders who had had warnings of the attack but had done little to prepare for it. The death and destruction at Pearl Harbor had been dealt out by the Japanese but there was also an element of American incompetence involved. So, all in all, it was better to wait until America had a few victories under her belt – and victories that had been filmed – before showing one of her greatest defeats.

If this was the reason for the ban, it was seriously flawed. Pearl Harbor in terms of myth and imagery was one of the best – if not the single most effective – American motivators of the whole war. The slogan "Remember Pearl Harbor" ran through hundreds of poster and recruiting campaigns. What is more, fairly early on in the war the US

government discovered that the response to colour films promoting war bonds was far greater than those shot in black and white. There is no doubt that Pearl Harbor in colour would have been a sell-out at the box office.

FRAME CLIPPED FROM AMATEUR MOVIE FILM OF USS *ARIZONA* EXPLODING DURING THE ATTACK ON PEARL HARBOR, DECEMBER 7, 1941.

The black-and-white footage of the attack was eventually released to the public in late 1942 and several newsreel films were made. In addition, the US government commissioned Hollywood film director John Ford to make a feature film of the raid. It was called *December 7th* and was also initially banned in its complete version because it suggested that the attack would have failed had the army and navy not been asleep on the job. A shorter less controversial version was released in 1943 but the American public had to wait until the 1990s to see the full, unedited version. In the film, Ford uses a mixture of real footage and staged scenes. There are actual shots of Japanese planes attacking American ships mixed in with models and re-enactments. Much of it was shot in colour in the Spring of 1942 with the damaged hulks of the US battleships still visible in the habour. Ford also went to great lengths and used sophisticated camera trickery – a bit crude by today's standards of special effects – to re-create the battle action of the raid. It was so realistic that many top navy bosses could not tell the difference. From a detailed study of this footage it can be seen that he had access to the lost colour footage; a few shots appear here and there, though sadly only in black and white.

Today all that appears to exist in the US National Archives in Washington of this extraordinary and historic footage is a series of very faded prints. Somewhere along the line the original colour master copies have gone missing. Following the trail back in time, they seem to have disappeared from the vaults of the Navy Photographic Centre in the mid-1960s, to be filed in another vault of "secret photographic imagery".

Over the years, there have been numerous attempts to track them down. In the late 1960s, Fox Studios, during the making of the film *Tora! Tora! Tora!* about the attack, reportedly offered a reward of $1 million, no questions asked, for the footage, but to no avail. In the 1990s, there was a navy-led investigation that included the FBI. It discovered that the seized colour film of the attack was supposed to have been returned to its original owners by the late 1940s, with copies being retained, first by John Ford's production team, then passed on to the navy and finally to the National Archives in the 1970s. It concluded that the colour originals had been lost or stolen. According to official files

the loss was not documented until 1968. The only other clue to their existence is that there are two colour stills in the National Archives collection that are frames – and marked as such – clipped or copied from Captain Hakansson's film. They are a tantalizing glimpse of what has been lost.

So what happened to this remarkable footage? Has it simply been lost or hidden away, forgotten in some secret vault or destroyed in some embarrassing accident or

ANOTHER FRAME CLIPPED FROM THE PEARL HARBOR FILM.

stolen by some ruthless and well-connected collector? Pearl Harbor was one of the most important events in US history. The fact that it was filmed at all is remarkable, but in colour is more extraordinary still. The loss of this unique record represents an unconscionable gap in America's documentary heritage, one that surely deserves a top-level congressional enquiry to discover the truth of the films' mysterious disappearance – and recover them for an eager public.

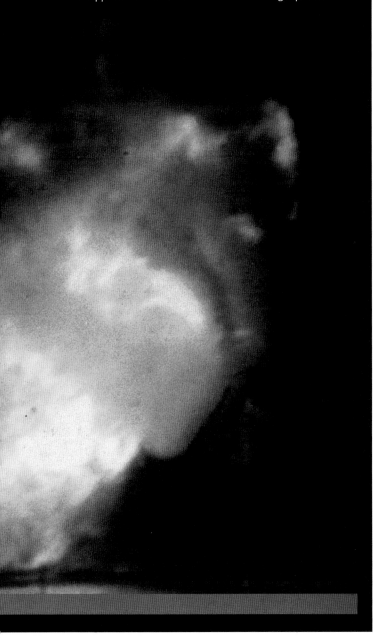

Many accounts of the attack on Pearl Harbor have attempted to excuse the Japanese for not declaring war first, explaining it away as a failure of communications between Tokyo and Washington. But surprise attacks were a part of Japanese military tradition dating back to Admiral Togo's pre-emptive strike on the Russian fleet at Port Arthur in 1904, and were also rooted in samurai history. There is even a samurai saying: "Win first, fight later". The surprise element at Pearl Harbor was entirely intentional and had one purpose – to strike a devastating blow against the US that would make America think twice about interfering in Japanese plans for the takeover of Asia. In the short term, it succeeded: within hours of the dawn attack, a meticulously planned campaign was launched against American, British and Dutch forces in the Philippines, Malaya, China and the East Indies. Tojo and his ministers hoped that once these territories had been captured, the Allies would sue for peace rather than fight a bloody war in distant lands.

But this strategy ultimately failed for two reasons. Firstly, the prime target – the American aircraft carriers – were not destroyed or even damaged as by chance they were not in Pearl Harbor at the time of the attack. Secondly, and more importantly, the Japanese government hugely underestimated American resolve. The surprise attack and the huge loss of life enraged the American government and public. It was a massively effective call to arms for the people, and once the American nation was properly mobilized in terms of its massive production power, the outcome of the war was never in doubt. It was simply a question of time.

The Japanese people first heard that the war in the Pacific had started when a breathless NHK (Japan's state broadcasting service) announcer read the 7 a.m. news: "We now bring you very urgent news. The army and navy departments of the Imperial General Headquarters jointly announced at six o'clock this morning, December 8, that the Imperial Army and Navy forces have begun hostilities against the American and British forces in the Pacific." The news was relayed throughout Japan on thousands of loudspeakers set up in the streets. Those who heard it were stunned into momentary silence, but as the news began to spread there was growing excitement. Some people clapped openly, others bowed in prayer towards the imperial palace.

The official declaration of war came in the form of an imperial rescript, a formal message from the emperor couched in almost impenetrable court language. It placed responsibility for the war squarely on the Americans and the British – "eager for the realization of their inordinate ambition to dominate the Orient" – and how "they have obstructed by every means our peaceful commerce ... menacing gravely the existence of our empire... The situation being such as it is, our empire for its existence and self-defence has no other recourse but to appeal to arms and to crush every obstacle in its path." It was carried on the front page of every newspaper and read out on the radio from then until the end of the war on the ninth day of every month just so no Japanese was in any doubt as to what the war was about.

Later that same day, Prime Minister Tojo made a speech broadcast on the radio:

JAPANESE FARMING FAMILY, C.1940S.

I am filled with awe and trepidation. Powerless as I am, I am resolved to dedicate myself, body and soul, and to set at ease the august mind of our sovereign. And I believe that every one of you, my fellow countrymen, will not care for your life but gladly share in the honour to make of yourself His Majesty's humble shield. The key to success lies in a faith in victory. For 2,600 years since it was founded, our empire has never known a defeat. This record alone is enough to produce a conviction in our ability to crush any enemy no matter how strong. Let us pledge ourselves that we will never stain our glorious history, but will go forward ... The rise or fall of our empire and the prosperity or ruin of East Asia literally depend upon the outcome of this war. Truly it is a time for the one hundred million of us Japanese to dedicate all we have and sacrifice everything for our country's cause. As long as there remains this great spirit of loyalty and patriotism, we have nothing to fear in fighting America and Britain. Victory, I am convinced, is always with the illustrious virtues of our sovereign. In making known these humble views of mine, I join with all my countrymen in pledging myself to assist in the grand imperial enterprise.

The broadcast was followed by the singing of a famous military song, "*Umi Yukaba*" that ended with the words,

Across the sea, corpses lie in the water;
Across the mountain, corpses lie in the fields.
I shall die only for the Emperor,
I shall never look back.

The most important part of Tojo's message was hidden away amid the patriotic rhetoric. Tojo didn't promise an easy, quick victory, in fact he foresaw a long and difficult road: "Our adversaries, boasting rich natural resources, aim at the domination of the world. In order to annihilate the enemy and to construct an unshakeable new order of East Asia, we should anticipate a long war." The fact was that anyone who was in the know realized the task ahead was almost impossible. Even Admiral Yamamoto, the genius behind the Pearl Harbor attack, had declared in 1940, "In the first six to twelve months of a war with the United States and Great Britain I will run wild and win victory upon victory. But then, if the war continues after that, I have no expectation of success."

SOLDIERS GET A BLESSING AT THE YASAKUNI SHRINE IN TOKYO BEFORE GOING TO THE FRONT, C.1930S.

# Chapter 6

# TRIUMPH AND DEFEAT

THE JAPANESE WAR PLAN WAS INITIALLY INCREDIBLY SUCCESSFUL AND DESERVES MUCH PRAISE FOR ITS AUDACITY AND THE EFFICIENCY WITH WHICH IT WAS CARRIED OUT OVER SUCH HUGE DISTANCES. THE IMPERIAL JAPANESE NAVY WENT ON TO PERFORM TWO MORE DARING ATTACKS: FIRSTLY ON THE AUSTRALIAN NAVY AT DARWIN ON FEBRUARY 19, 1942, SINKING SIX SHIPS INCLUDING AN AMERICAN DESTROYER, DESTROYING SCORES OF AIRCRAFT AND KILLING 243 PEOPLE; THE SAME FORCE THEN WENT ON TO ATTACK THE BRITISH FLEET BASED AT TRINCOMALEE AND COLOMBO IN CEYLON WITH EVEN MORE EFFECT. IN A SERIES OF RAIDS BETWEEN APRIL 5–9, JAPANESE CARRIER PLANES SANK TWO CRUISERS, TWO DESTROYERS, THE AIRCRAFT CARRIER *HERMES* AND KILLED OVER 800 SAILORS.

On land, the Japanese army was even more successful. Within four months of Pearl Harbor, Japan had conquered Malaya, Singapore, the Dutch East Indies, the Philippines, and scores of other islands belonging to the Western powers. They had invaded Burma and were close to the border with India. Japanese forces seemed poised to conquer almost the entire Pacific basin and even invade Australia and New Zealand. In almost all cases, the Allied commanders were caught by complete surprise by the speed and ferocity of the Japanese attacks and many were forced into humiliating surrenders.

The war in the Pacific did not actually start with the attack on Pearl Harbor; it began with the invasion of Malaya. Very early in the morning on December 7 Japanese ships approached the Malay peninsula and, two hours before the first planes attacked the American fleet in Hawaii, the bombardment began. The invasion plan involved three separate attacks, two on the coast of Thailand and one on Malaya itself. They encountered little effective resistance and by the end of the day the Japanese troops were safely ashore and pushing south towards their ultimate goal and the major symbol of British imperialism in the Far East, the fortress of Singapore.

Singapore's inhabitants first learned of the Japanese invasion with an air raid at four o'clock in the morning. It achieved complete surprise and no British fighters got airborne to oppose it. The city's lights remained on throughout the raid as the man responsible for electricity could not be found. Despite the deaths of 63 people and a further 133 injured, the British

ABOVE: JAPANESE ARMY FIGHTING IN CHINA, 1937.
TOP LEFT: USS *MISSISSINEWA* BURNS FIERCELY AFTER BEING HIT BY A *KAITEN*, OR HUMAN TORPEDO, ON NOVEMBER 20, 1944.

commanders and the colony's inhabitants remained supremely confident that they could defeat the Japanese invaders, particularly as two powerful British warships, HMS *Repulse* and HMS *Prince of Wales* had recently arrived to bolster the island's defences. Air Chief Marshal Sir Robert Brooke-Popham, the British Commander-in-Chief in the Far East, issued an order of the day: "We are ready. We have had plenty of warning and our preparations are made and tested. We are confident. Our defences are strong and our weapons are efficient." He was to be wrong on all accounts. The British and Commonwealth troops were not ready, their defences were ill prepared and their weapons were inadequate to face the Japanese onslaught. In particular, there were no British tanks in the peninsula as it was thought they were ill suited to jungle warfare, and the Brewster Buffalo fighter planes assigned to protect the colony's airspace were a poor match for the Japanese Zeros. British commanders were also lacking compared to their Japanese opponents.

The first British mistake was to send out the two big ships in an effort to destroy the Japanese invasion convoys, but without any proper air cover. The commander of Force Z, Admiral "Tom Thumb" Phillips (so-called because of his diminutive size), asked several times for fighters to protect his ships but he was told it was impossible as the forward airfields had already been captured by the Japanese. The two capital ships and their destroyer escorts would have to cope on their own. They sailed from Singapore on the afternoon of December 8, proud symbols of British naval power whose vulnerability was about to be cruelly exposed.

RAF BREWSTER BUFFALO FIGHTERS DESTROYED ON THE GROUND DURING THE MALAYAN CAMPAIGN, 1942.

The cruiser and the battleship were almost immediately spotted by a Japanese submarine and their position and course passed on to the headquarters of the Imperial Japanese Navy's 22nd Air Flotilla in Saigon. Just after 11 a.m. on December 10, the Japanese planes found them and their bombs and torpedoes soon started finding their mark. The *Repulse* was the first to be hit, by a dive bomber. The *Prince of Wales* had her steering mechanism damaged and she started listing to port. The *Repulse* was the first to go down, rolling over and sinking stern first at 12.33 p.m., followed by the *Prince of Wales* about 45 minutes later. Captain John Leach and Admiral Phillips both went down with their ships, along with over 800 British seamen. The pride of the Royal Navy, known affectionately as "HMS *Unsinkable*" had been sunk and with it one of the best hopes of saving the British forces in Malaya. Of the 84 attacking Japanese aircraft only three were shot down. It was an ominous sign for the defenders of Singapore.

JAPANESE POSITIONS ON KEWKONG ROAD IN SHANGHAI, AUGUST 1937.

By the time of the demise of Force Z, the Japanese army was already pouring down the peninsula of Malaya. Despite being outnumbered almost two to one, each time the Japanese came across a British line of defence, they either outflanked it or burst through with their tanks, against which the poorly equipped British had almost no defence. By January 7, they had crossed the strategically important Slim River and were less than 250 miles from Singapore itself. The British and Commonwealth troops were now in complete disarray and General Wavell ordered a full withdrawal south. There was now almost nothing between the Japanese army and its intended prize of Singapore, and the island's defences against a landward attack were practically non-existent. By January 31, all British and Commonwealth forces had crossed the narrow shallow channel between the mainland of Malaya and the island of Singapore and the last bridge was blown up. Singapore was now isolated, the last bulwark of the British Empire in the Far East.

AUSTRALIAN POWS WORKING ON A BRIDGE IN MALAYA, 1942.

The most important British base in the Far East, along with an army of over 130,000 British and Empire troops, had fallen to a Japanese force barely half its size. It was the most humiliating defeat in British military history and the Japanese army's greatest victory. Above all, it was a decisive blow against the domination of Asia by the white man. Japan was now the master of Asia and there was nothing the British could do about it. In the days that followed, the Japanese press went wild. The *Asahi Shimbun* was typical when its special correspondent in Singapore wrote on February 27, 1942, "In this city once filled with their glory, now the British prisoners are walking like zombies, downhearted and beaten... 120 years ago, Sir Stamford Raffles won an heroic victory here but now under the gaze of his statue, the dream of empire cannot last much longer ... Did he ever expect to see the end of that dream?"

The campaign in Malaya and Singapore also gave the Allies a foretaste of the Japanese way of warfare. It had been fast, furious and cruel in the extreme. Prisoners had been beaten and murdered. Wounded patients and nurses at the Alexandra Military Hospital in Singapore were killed in cold blood. During the occupation large numbers of Chinese were rounded up and disappeared, presumed murdered. The exact numbers remain a mystery, but estimates range from 8,000 to over 50,000. The surrendered British forces fared little better. They were made to work as slave labour, building a railway in the disease-ridden jungles of Burma and Thailand. Over 16,000 died before the war's end.

The extraordinary speed and extent of their early successes caught Japanese commanders by surprise. They had not expected the Allies to collapse so quickly but more importantly the hoped-for negotiated peace had also not materialized. In fact both Roosevelt and Churchill were sounding more belligerent than ever and had vowed that the war would go on until total Allied victory was achieved. American citizens of Japanese descent were rounded up and sent to remote internment camps. A massive American naval building programme was launched. Peace was the last thing on the Allies' minds.

In April 1942, war came to the people of Japan themselves. In an extraordinarily daring raid from an aircraft carrier in the middle of the Pacific, 16 American B-25 bombers, led by Colonel Doolittle, bombed the cities of Tokyo, Osaka, Nagoya and Kobe. It was done partly as revenge for Pearl Harbor and partly as a means of bolstering US morale. The raid did little physical damage but the psychological effect on the Japanese people was important, especially as it was the first time their homeland had come under substantial attack for over 1000 years. A Japanese newspaper described the raiders as "demons who carried out an inhuman, insatiable, indiscriminate bombing attack on the sly". For the Americans it was a one-way mission as they were at the very limit of their flying range. The crews either crash-landed or bailed out over China and Russia. The Japanese executed three of the aircrew whom they captured, and killed an estimated 25,000 Chinese soldiers and civilians in areas where the aircraft landed.

With the war against the Allies barely six months old, things started to go wrong for the Japanese. In an attempt to conquer New Guinea, the Japanese suffered their first setback at the Battle of the Coral Sea, when two aircraft carriers were badly damaged for the loss of one American. The Japanese high command described the battle as a victory but the failure to secure New Guinea was to have dire consequences for the Japanese, whereas the loss of one aircraft carrier would have little impact on Allied fortunes.

COLONEL JAMES H. DOOLITTLE, COMMANDER OF THE RAID BY 16 B-25 BOMBERS ON JAPAN IN APRIL 1942.

ABOVE: A SHINTO PRIEST LEADS A PARADE OF POLITICIANS AND ARMY OFFICERS THROUGH TOKYO. OVERLEAF: EMPIRE DAY AT THE YASUKUNI SHRINE, C.1930s.

On the home front, things became almost as bad. People were bombarded with slogans such as "One hundred million people, one mind", "Abolish desire until victory", "Deny oneself and serve the nation" and "Luxury is the enemy". There were frequent government campaigns aimed at encouraging frugality and austerity, such as the wearing of utilitarian trousers or *Monpe* instead of the traditional kimono, and campaigns against unpatriotic Western fashions. At the start of the war, every family in Japan was encouraged to join one of the newly formed neighbourhood associations (*tonarigumi*), controlled by the Home Ministry. Each association consisted of between five and ten households living in close proximity. They were intended to ensure that all wartime regulations were followed and that everyone donated generously in time and money to the national war effort. Membership of these associations was soon made obligatory and their duties were formalized to include the distribution of rations, air defence, the coordination of savings drives and volunteer labour, and ensuring that men eligible for the draft reported for duty. The system relied on the fact that even if people were willing to cheat the government, they would not cheat their neighbours.

Rice rationing began in Tokyo and other large cities even before Pearl Harbor, on April 1, 1940. Other basics such as miso and soy sauce were rationed from February 1942. Soon after that almost everything was rationed and in short supply. By the end of the war, a survey showed that the daily calorie level of the average Japanese had dropped from 2,400 to just 1,800 calories, far less than in the other defeated Axis nations. The Economic Mobilization Law of 1938 had created a command economy in which the government could control industry and decide what was produced and where. Inevitably, as the war situation deteriorated, this meant that the production of anything other than war goods was severely limited. The Ministry of Commerce and Industry brought in a coupon system for clothing on February 1, 1942, limiting each person living in a city to 100 points a year, while those living in the countryside had to survive on just 80 points. A blouse was eight points, a pair of socks two points and a man's overcoat fifty points. As the war progressed the points total was reduced and the "cost" of items increased, but in reality things just disappeared from the shops.

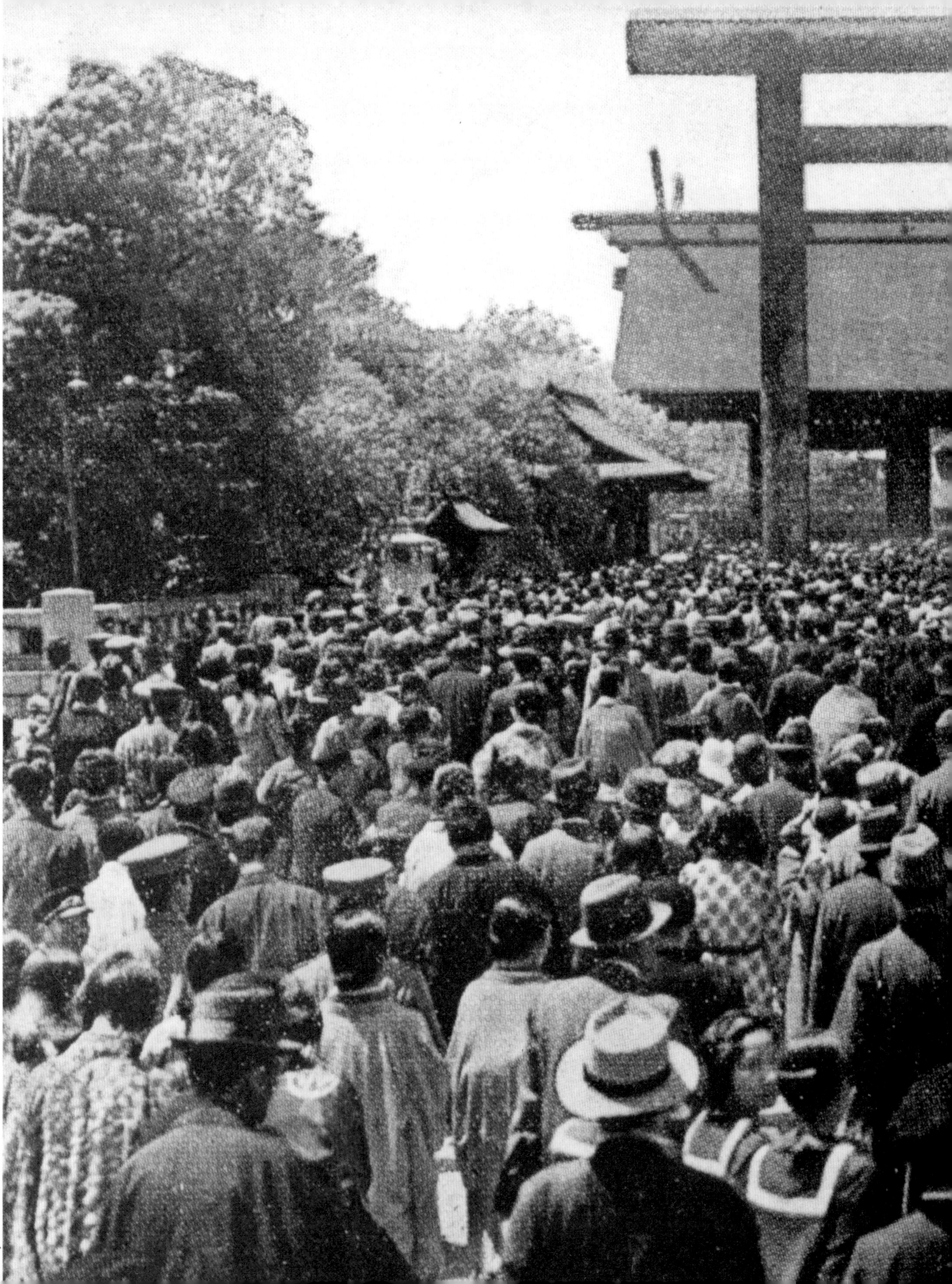

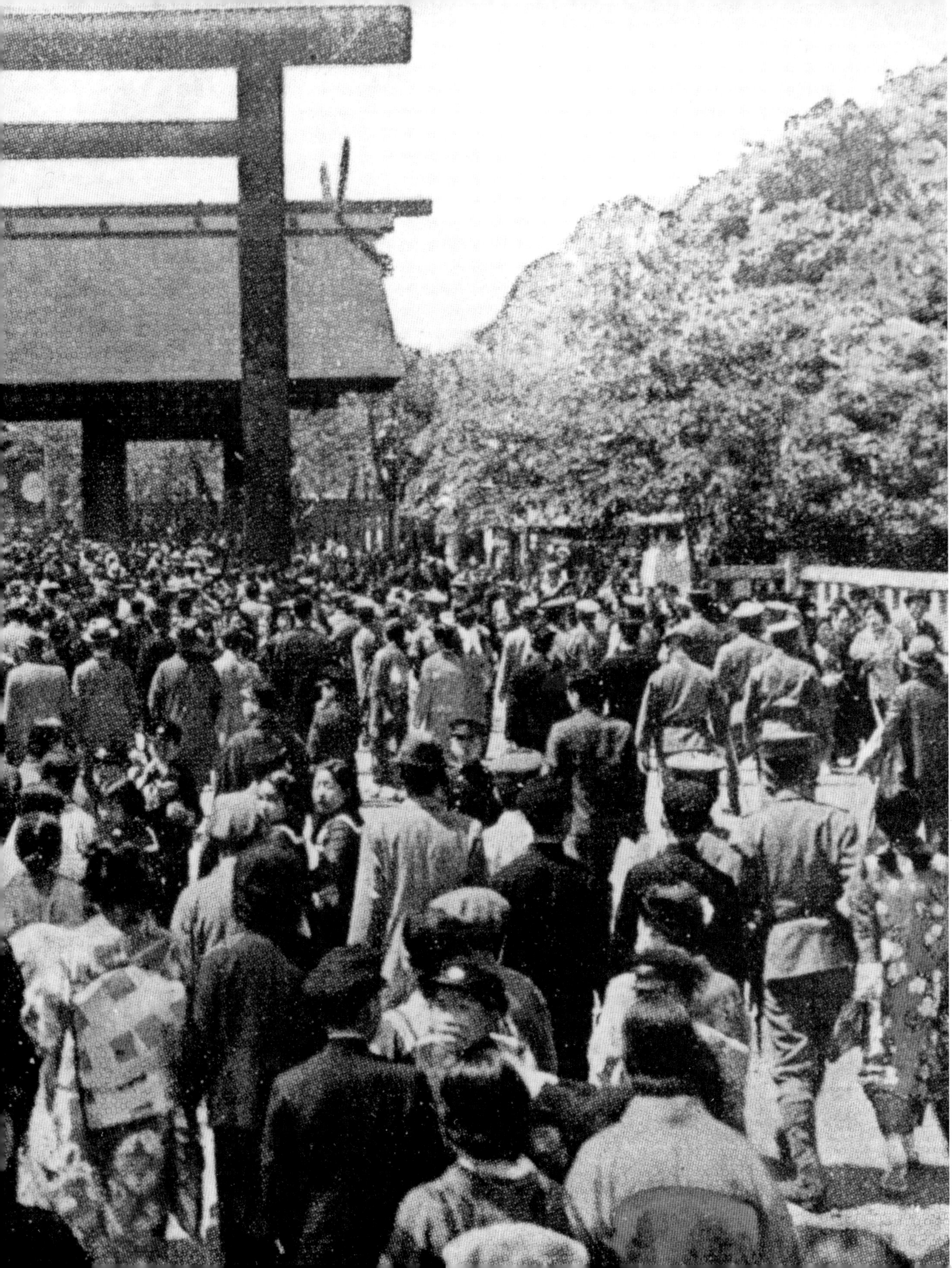

## THE JAPANESE FIGHTING CODE

In January 1941 the Japanese army issued a new field service code to regulate military life both on and off the field of battle. It began by stating:

The battlefield is where the Imperial Army, acting under the imperial command, displays its true character, conquering wherever it attacks, winning whenever it engages in combat, in order to spread "The Imperial Way", whereby the Japanese people, achieving a unity of mind, with the emperor as master and serving him with loyalty and devotion, endeavour to establish a highly moral nation through whose moral influence they hope to contribute to the peace and welfare of the world far and wide so that the enemy may look up in awe to the august virtues of His Majesty. Those who march to the battlefield, therefore, should exalt throughout the world the glories of the empire by fully realizing what the country stands for and firmly upholding the moral tenets of the Imperial Army.

It had seven sections: "The Empire", "The Imperial Army", "Discipline", "Unity", "Cooperation", "Aggressiveness" and "The Conviction to Win". In the section on the Imperial Army it stated:

Valour requires strictness, while benevolence must be universal. Should there be an enemy who dares to oppose the Imperial Army, the army must resolutely resort to force of arms and deal him a crushing blow. However, even though force may compel the enemy to submit, should a lapse in virtue occur by the striking of those who do not resist or by a failure to show kindness to those who surrender, it cannot be said that such an army is always perfect.

Life for the Japanese soldier or sailor was brutal. Officers regularly resorted to violence to enforce obedience without fear of retribution. Letters and diaries recall beatings for the most trivial of matters, such as serving an officer's rice too slowly or using a vest as a towel. The service code emphasized that obedience had to be absolute, even if it meant death: "The spirit of the soldier is best exemplified by those who silently do their duty, joyfully braving death in obedience to a command given at a time when they are undergoing great hardships." It went on to explain that the individual didn't matter; it was the survival of the unit that counted: "It is essential that each man, of both high and low rank, dutifully observing his place, should be determined always to sacrifice himself for the whole, in accordance with the intentions of the commander, by reposing every confidence in his comrades, and without giving even the slightest thought to personal interest and to life or death."

In battle the code extolled aggression: "When attacking, be determined and positive, always taking the initiative, fighting vigorously and stubbornly, vowing not to cease until the enemy is crushed. In defence, always retain the spirit of attack and always maintain freedom of action; never give up a position but rather die. In pursuit, be thorough and inexorable." Most famously, it exhorted all Japanese soldiers never to surrender: "The destiny of the empire rests upon victory or defeat in battle. Do not give up under any circumstances, keeping in mind your responsibility not to tarnish the glorious history of the Imperial Army with its tradition of invincibility." The code ended with a solemn demand that every Japanese would understand: "Meet the expectations of your family and home community by making effort upon effort, always mindful of the honour of your name. If alive, do not suffer the disgrace of becoming a prisoner; in death, do not leave behind a name soiled by misdeeds." Surrender had always been regarded as deeply shameful in Japanese society. Returning Japanese POWs from the Russian war of 1904–05 were treated as social outcasts. As a result, there were almost no Japanese mass surrenders until the very end of the war. Every battle was a fight to the death.

On the Island of Saipan, less than 10% of the Japanese garrison of 29,000 surrendered to US forces in July 1944.

As with all US island invasions, it was preceded by a massive bombardment from battleships, cruisers, destroyers and rocket ships. Then the dive-bombers went in, 155 of them in the first wave. Despite all this, when the Marines hit the beaches – 8,000 landed in the first 20 minutes – the Japanese were far from defeated. Almost every inch of the island had to be contested, blasted with high explosive, scorched with flame-throwers and then fought over hand-to-hand and even then the defenders still refused to surrender. Japanese counter-attacks, often in the form of suicide charges, increased the slaughter on both sides. Saipan was just too important to give up.

When news of the American invasion of Saipan reached Tokyo, Imperial Headquarters sent an urgent message to Admiral Ozawa, commander of the Japanese Mobile Fleet operating in the seas off New Guinea. He was ordered to attack the US fleet in the Marianas at any cost. At the end of the message, the famous phrase used by the Japanese hero of the Russo-Japanese War, Admiral Togo, was added, akin to Nelson's famous message to his fleet before Trafalgar: "The rise and fall of Imperial Japan depends on this one battle.

Every man shall do his utmost." The Japanese fleet was vastly outnumbered in aircraft carriers, and the extra land-based aircraft hoped for from the Marianas had already been destroyed by the Americans. The US pilots were also flying a new plane, the Hellcat, which could out-climb and out-dive the ageing Zero. What came next was the most comprehensive defeat of Japanese naval air power in the entire war. In just a few hours, almost 250 Japanese planes and their pilots were shot down for the loss of just 29 US planes. To complete the defeat, American submarines spotted the Japanese fleet and sank two carriers. The American carriers then launched their own bombers and torpedo planes and sank another carrier. The Japanese navy would never recover from the Battle of the Philippine Sea, or, as the Americans liked to call it, the Great Marianas Turkey Shoot.

Saipan's fate was now sealed, although it had never been in any real doubt. By June 25, there were barely 1,000 unwounded Japanese soldiers left fighting. Five days later, the Japanese commander, General Saito, wrote a message to his surviving troops which ended:

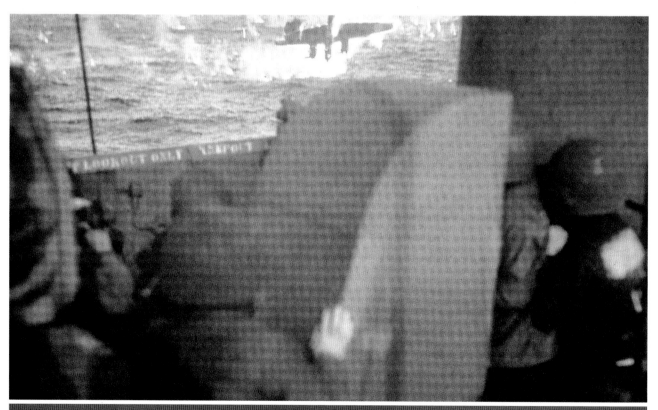

A KAMIKAZE PLANE IS SHOT DOWN OFF OKINAWA, APRIL 1945.

US Sherman tank with flamethrower, 1944.

Our comrades have fallen one after another. Despite the bitterness of defeat we pledge, "Seven lives to repay our country"... Whether we attack or whether we stay where we are, there is only death. However in death, there is life. We must utilize this opportunity to exalt true Japanese manhood. I will advance with those who remain to deliver still another blow to the American devils and leave my bones on Saipan as a bulwark of the Pacific ... I will never suffer the disgrace of being taken alive and I will offer up the courage of my soul and calmly rejoice in living by the eternal principle. Here I pray with you for the eternal life of the emperor and the welfare of the country and I advance to seek out the enemy. Follow me.

General Saito and his staff then asked some young officers to help them commit suicide by shooting them in the back of the head. The remaining Japanese soldiers and some civilians joined together in one last suicide charge. They ran headlong into 800 men of the 1st and 2nd Battalions of the 105th Infantry Regiment of the 27th US Marine Division. The slaughter was incredible but the charge almost overwhelmed the Marines; only the timely intervention of some tanks decided the battle. Two days later the island was declared secure. Over 27,000 Japanese and more than 3,000 American soldiers lay dead.

There was one final horror to come before the battle for Saipan was over. Hundreds of Japanese civilians stranded in Saipan by the invasion had been driven into the northern tip of the island by the American advance. They now gathered at the top of high cliffs. Despite the best efforts of Japanese interpreters, many refused to listen to reason and threw themselves to their deaths or blew themselves up with hand grenades. One of the most memorable – and tragic – images of the entire Pacific war was that of a Japanese mother hurling her baby off the cliff top before jumping to her own death. As the Americans invaded the rest of the Japanese-held Pacific, they would encounter more of these group suicides or *gyokusai* which translates literally as "the breaking of a jewel" and signifies the destruction of a precious young life for the sake of honour and loyalty to Japan.

THE ISLAND OF TARAWA UNDER ATTACK BY JAPANESE BOMBERS, DECEMBER 1943.

Back home, the Japanese people were kept in the dark about the rapidly worsening war situation. Since the Battle of Midway government propagandists had attempted to continue the story of victory with clever lies about the level of Japanese and American losses, but as time went on their claims became less believable. In particular the loss of Saipan was difficult to hide. It was not a recently conquered territory, a piece of the new empire which could be given up for military reasons. As part of the old German Mariana Islands, it had been integrated into the empire during the First World War. Japan had officially been granted a mandate over the islands in 1920. Thousands of Japanese had made the island their home; to all intents and purposes it was a part of the Japanese homeland, and now it had fallen. Prime Minister Tojo had staked his political future on the fate of Saipan so when it fell, he had to go. Two days before handing the Emperor his resignation, Tojo made a speech in which he said, "Let all of us one hundred million people together renew our pledge and our determination to make the supreme sacrifice and concentrate the traditional fighting spirit of our country handed down through three thousand years to the attainment of the ultimate victory, thereby setting the mind of His Imperial Majesty at rest."

If the Battle of Midway had been the military turning point of the Pacific War, the fall of Saipan was a major psychological turning point for the Japanese people. Its full significance was only fully appreciated in November when the first American B-29 bombers took off from the repaired and extended airstrip and began the sustained bombing of Japan. From now on no one and nowhere was safe. It was total war for everyone in Japan. And total war demanded a desperate response.

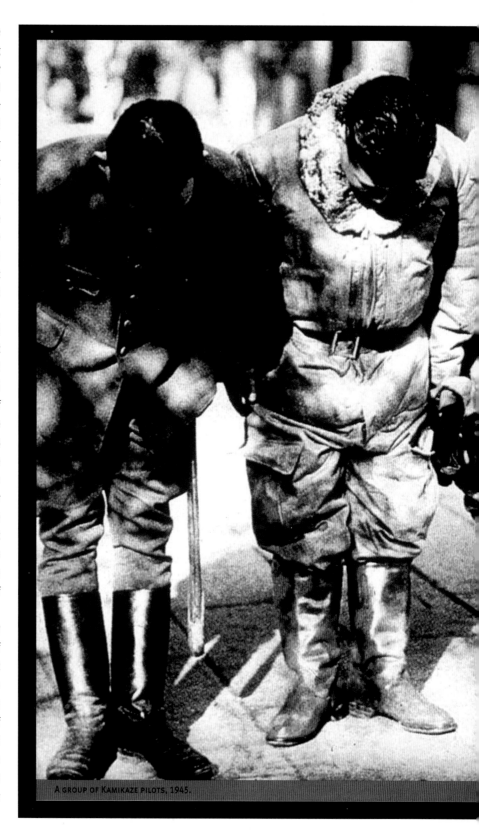

A GROUP OF KAMIKAZE PILOTS, 1945.

## DIVINE WIND

In blossom today, then scattered;
Life is so like a delicate flower.
How can one expect the fragrance
To last forever?

This is a haiku composed by Admiral Takijiro Onishi, one of the founders of the infamous Kamikaze corps. The symbolism of the blossom dates back to the time of the samurai, who believed that they should be prepared to sacrifice their lives for their lords just as the cherry blossom drops at the faintest breath of wind.

Kamikaze pilots have featured heavily in many accounts of Japan's defeat in the Second World War. Someone prepared to crash his plane into a ship and kill himself has come to symbolize the utter desperation of the Japanese cause as the war situation deteriorated. Kamikaze itself means divine wind and derives from the name given to a heaven-sent typhoon that devastated a Mongol fleet in the thirteenth century, the last time Japan had faced an invading enemy. And so the name was now given to the young men who would fly like the wind and drive away the barbarian hordes that threatened to invade Japan in 1945.

Suicidal death in combat has a long tradition in Japan. The samurai followed a code that in certain situations demanded they kill themselves by ritual disembowelment – *seppuku*. In more recent times there were many stories of Japanese soldiers hurling themselves suicidally at enemy positions in both the Russo-Japanese and Sino-Japanese wars. In the early part of the Second World War there were also several instances of individual Japanese pilots crashing their craft into enemy planes to bring them down, but it was only in the last eighteen months of the war that there was an official suicide policy and a special corps dedicated to it.

When people think of the bombing of Japan during the Second World War they understandably recall the appalling devastation caused by the atomic bombs dropped on Hiroshima and Nagasaki in August 1945. The exact number of immediate deaths is impossible to calculate with any certainty but estimates range from 100,000–200,000 killed in the two blasts. Almost 200,000 Japanese had also been killed in the 'conventional' bombing of hundreds of Japanese cities by the Americans. By the time the two A-bombs were dropped, Japan had been under air attack for over ten months by US B-29s stationed in the Mariana Islands, and since February 1945, it had been under firebomb attack, one of the deadliest and most destructive weapons ever devised. Napalm was widely used during these attacks. Developed by DuPont and Standard Oil, napalm is a compound of jellied gasoline that sticks to almost anything, and burns slowly and with high intensity so that fires spread. It was particularly effective against the wood and paper buildings in Japanese cities.

The bomber that delivered this death and destruction was the B-29 Superfortress. It had four massive 2,200-horsepower engines, each turning a 16-foot, 6-inch propeller. The plane weighed 74,500 pounds and had a maximum speed of 357 miles per hour. With a wingspan of 141 feet, 3 inches it was the biggest aircraft of the war, and it contained some of the most sophisticated aircraft technology of the time including a central fire-control system and remotely controlled machine guns. Perhaps its greatest asset was its operating range of 3,800 miles that allowed the Americans to take the war to the Japanese people themselves.

During 1943–44, the US Air Force had followed a policy of precision bombing, but by the end of 1944 it became apparent that this was not causing significant damage to Japanese industry or morale. In early 1945, the air force was authorized to begin the firebombing of the Japanese mainland. The scale of operations was stepped up with the arrival of General Curtis LeMay to command the 21st Bomber Command on the Mariana Islands. The B-29s were switched to night attacks, at altitudes of around 7,000 feet, on the major population centres of Tokyo, Nagoya, Osaka and Kobe. The rationale given at the time for a shift from mostly industrial or military to civilian targets was the belief that much of Japanese war production had been moved from large-scale plants to small factories and workshops within the cities. This was certainly true, but there is no doubt that General LeMay was also determined to use firebombs against the largely wood-built Japanese cities in an effort to break Japanese morale. Despite

ABOVE: A B-29 BOMBER DROPPING FIREBOMBS, 1945.

the widespread destruction and loss of life, this never happened; the Japanese population, like their German allies, remained remarkably resilient throughout the bombing campaign.

The first firebomb raid was on the city of Kobe on February 3, 1945. It was deemed a success and so the scope of the raids was widened. In the end over 60 Japanese cities were attacked in this way. The B-29s were modified, with much of their armour and defensive weapons being removed to allow increased bomb loads, as by this stage of the war Japanese air defences aircraft were so feeble as to make the risk of being shot down relatively light. Tokyo was first firebombed on the night of February 23–24 when 174 B-29s destroyed approximately one square mile of the city. Then on the night of March 9–10 came the biggest and most destructive raid on the capital with an attack by 334 Superfortresses. Pathfinder planes flew over the city on intersecting courses, dropping one napalm bomb every 100 feet and the following main bomber force saw Tokyo with a massive burning X in its centre. For the next three hours waves of B-29s dropped their loads of napalm on the people of Tokyo. The fires were soon out of control; there was little the Tokyo fire crews could do and in any case they ran out of water. What made matters worse that night was a strong wind that fanned the flames into a massive all-devouring firestorm that sucked the life out of the city and incinerated anyone left within. Even the water in Tokyo's rivers reached boiling point. The fire was so intense that it created updraughts that tossed the gigantic B-29s around like leaves. Fourteen bombers were lost in the raid and 42 damaged but the toll they inflicted was enormous. More than 100,000 people died and 265,171 buildings in almost 16 square miles of the city were reduced to ashes. The next morning the city streets were filled with the still-smouldering bodies. And this was only the beginning; in the next ten days, B-29s destroyed more than 32 square miles of urban Japan.

April 1945 was a relatively quiet month for the cities as many of the B-29s were diverted to bomb bases launching Kamikaze attacks on the US Navy off Okinawa. Nevertheless, by the end of the month, a further 17 square miles of Tokyo had gone up in flames and in addition approximately 3.5 square miles of Kawasaki and 1.5 square miles of Yokohama had suffered the same fate.

In May the B-29s returned with a vengeance. Nagoya was targeted, with four square miles gutted by fire. Tokyo was hit again, with the financial, commercial and government districts as the prime targets, and another 17 square miles of the capital went up in flames. The attacks had now almost halved the size of Tokyo, with a total of 56 square miles in ruins. Even the Imperial Palace had been hit, albeit accidentally, as the US pilots had specific orders to avoid it. The key port of Yokohama was again firebombed at the end of May, and nine square miles of the city's industrial and commercial areas were destroyed. In Osaka, Japan's second biggest city, a further 136,107 houses and 4,222 factories were destroyed.

By this late stage of the war, plans were being finalized for the invasion of Japan itself and the projected estimates of American casualties ranged up to 100,000. It was hoped that the bombing might bring about Japan's surrender without invasion, so in June and July 1945 the B-29 raids were intensified still further. General LeMay now widened his list of targets to include many smaller towns as most of the large cities were already devastated. Many lost 50% or more of their buildings.

SURVIVOR IN THE RUINS OF TOKYO, 1945.

TOKYO IN RUINS AFTER FIREBOMB RAIDS, 1945.

Toyama, a town of 128,000 people, suffered almost 100% destruction; hardly a single building was left standing once the fires had eventually burnt out.

By the end of July 1945, the B-29s were literally running out of targets, but five cities still remained off the target list: Kyoto was spared as the cultural and historical capital of Japan while Niigata, Kokura, Nagasaki and Hiroshima – were being kept as targets for another, even more deadly weapon, the A-bomb.

In the final reckoning at the end of the war, the B-29s based in China and the Marianas had flown 33,000 sorties and had dropped over 168,000 tons of bombs, 63 per cent of which were firebombs. In comparison, American losses were small: only 414 B-29s shot down or destroyed and 2,148 American aircrew killed.

In total more than 200,000 people died in these bombing raids and an estimated 2.2 million Japanese homes were destroyed. Although more people were killed in the Allied bombing of Germany – and it lasted more than twice as long as the bombing of Japan – the destruction in Japan was far more widespread. Of Japan's major cities, Nagoya was 40% destroyed, Yokohama 58% destroyed, Kobe had lost 56% of its area and Osaka 35%. Japan's urban landscape had been almost obliterated.

**DAMAGE IN TOKYO FROM FIREBOMB RAIDS, 1945.**

# Chapter 7

# ENDURING THE UNENDURABLE

By THE SUMMER OF 1945, JAPAN WAS GOVERNED – STILL IN THE NAME OF THE EMPEROR – BY A SUPREME WAR COUNCIL OR "BIG SIX". THE COUNCIL WAS MADE UP OF REPRESENTATIVES OF THE ARMY, THE NAVY AND THE CIVILIAN GOVERNMENT AND WAS SUPPOSED TO OPERATE BY CONSENSUS, WHICH MEANT THAT THEY DEBATED AMONG THEMSELVES UNTIL THEY AGREED ON A COURSE OF ACTION WHICH WOULD THEN BE PRESENTED TO THE EMPEROR FOR HIS APPROVAL. THE MOST POWERFUL PERSON ON THE COUNCIL WAS THE WAR MINISTER. FROM EVEN BEFORE THE WAR, IT HAD BEEN ACCEPTED THAT NO WAR MINISTER COULD BE APPOINTED WITHOUT THE ARMY'S APPROVAL, AND NO GOVERNMENT COULD CONTINUE WITHOUT A WAR MINISTER. IN OTHER WORDS THE ARMY WAS IN DE FACTO CONTROL OF THE GOVERNMENT.

In August 1945, the major issue to be debated at the supreme war council was surrender but despite a heated and prolonged debate, the council could not reach consensus. They were split down the middle between those advocating a last-ditch defence of the homeland in the hope of forcing the Allies to concede better peace terms, and those who felt the only option was an unconditional surrender. The surrender faction comprised the prime minister, the 77-year-old and very frail Admiral Suzuki, Foreign Minister Togo and the navy minister, Admiral Yonai. The fight-to-the-death party was led by the war minister, General Anami, supported by Genera Umezu, the army chief of staff and Admiral Toyoda, navy chief of staff.

By this stage of the war, the emperor was also in favour of peace as long as it meant a continuation of the imperial system. In theory Hirohito could have simply ordered the army and navy to lay down their arms and surrender to the Allies. But it was not certain that the entire army would obey him. Also any attempt by him to intervene in politics could damage the reputation of the imperial throne, with serious consequences for his continued role as head of state. So for the time being he remained aloof from the debate.

This debate was taking place against the background of the Allies' Potsdam Declaration on July 26, which had again demanded the unconditional surrender of the entire Japanese nation before peace could be declared. The policy had first been agreed by the Allies at the Casablanca Conference in 1943 and they had never wavered from it.

CHURCHILL, ROOSEVELT AND STALIN MEET AT THE YALTA CONFERENCE IN FEBRUARY 1945.

One of the biggest sticking points for both doves and hawks was the future of the emperor himself. Would unconditional surrender result in the end of the imperial system? If so, in everyone's eyes that would mean the end of Japan as they knew it. The "hawks" believed the Allies were bent on ridding Japan of the emperor, the "doves" were not so sure. While the Japanese government prevaricated, the Allies acted. Hiroshima and Nagasaki were followed by warnings that further A-bombs would be dropped until unconditional surrender was agreed. And the Russian armies were soon rampaging through the demoralized Japanese forces in Manchuria. There were even suggestions that Tokyo might be the next target for an A-bomb. This information had been beaten out of an unfortunate American fighter pilot who had recently been shot down. He actually knew nothing, and had simply blurted "Tokyo" in the hope of getting his torturers to stop.

As the Big Six could not agree, the prime minister called a full cabinet meeting, but it too was split so on the night of August 9 an Imperial Conference was called. Again all the arguments were heard but still ministers remained divided. At approximately two o'clock in the morning, with all his ministers standing rigidly to attention after having bowed formally towards him, the emperor finally spoke:

I have given serious thought to the situation prevailing at home and abroad and have concluded that continuing the war can only mean destruction for the nation and prolongation of bloodshed and cruelty in the world ... It goes without saying that it is unbearable for me to see the brave and loyal fighting men of Japan disarmed. It is equally unbearable that others who have rendered me devoted service should now be punished as instigators of the war. Nevertheless the time has come when we must endure the unendurable ... I swallow my own tears and give my sanction to the proposal to accept the Allied proclamation.

JAPANESE OFFICERS SURRENDER AT YOKOSUKA NAVAL BASE, AUGUST 1945.

An hour later the Japanese government adopted the emperor's decision and a message was sent to the Allies via Sweden and Switzerland that Japan would accept the Potsdam Declaration as long as it did not "comprise any demand which prejudices the prerogatives of His Majesty as a sovereign ruler". As if to remind the Japanese of the realities of their desperate situation, on the morning of August 11, the Americans launched another bombing raid on the capital. It would be the last of the war.

Meanwhile, news had leaked out that surrender negotiations were underway and a group of diehard young army officers began to plot a coup to prevent it. The US response arrived very early in the morning of August 12. Unfortunately, in translation it seemed to suggest the Allies would make the emperor "subject" to the occupying authorities, something unthinkable in Japan. So the surrender-or-fight-to-the-death debate broke out once more.

Rumours of an impending coup were now flying around Tokyo. The hawks, especially General Anami, wanted to use the threat of a coup to persuade the doves on the supreme war council to renegotiate with the Allies. On August 14 Hirohito once more called all his ministers together and at a highly charged conference told them once again they should accept the Allies' demands and prepare an announcement for him to make to that effect. He and his closest advisers hoped that hearing him speak for the first time would stifle any attempt at rebellion. A formal rescript was prepared and Hirohito recorded it with NHK

engineers onto a waxed disc. That night General Anami returned home and committed *seppuku* while the rebellious officers put their plans for revolt into action. They murdered the commander of the Imperial Guards and forged his signature on an order. With it they managed to persuade some units of the Imperial Guards Division guarding the imperial palace to revolt. The coup leaders then attempted to assassinate all the doves, including Prime Minister Suzuki, but he managed to escape unharmed. When the rebels heard that the emperor had made a "surrender" recording, a detachment was sent to the palace to find and destroy it. Hirohito's advisers had anticipated this and hidden it in a maid's cupboard. Luckily for Japan and the world, it remained hidden.

The next day, the rebels' plans began to come unstuck when the commander of the Eastern District Army, General Tanaka, refused to join them. He went to the palace and ordered the guards to give up the rebellion. The coup attempt then collapsed and the young officers killed themselves in front of the palace.

At noon on August 15, 1945, the Emperor's voice was heard on radio for the first time. He said that Japan was ending the war "in order to save mankind" from nuclear oblivion. The speech was relayed around the embattled empire by short-wave radio. Many Japanese could barely hear through the static nor understand fully the complicated court language, but it was soon clear that the decision had been taken to surrender and that the war was finally over. It was a highly charged and emotional moment for

OFFICIAL JAPANESE DELEGATION AT THE FORMAL SIGNING OF SURRENDER ON USS *MISSOURI*, SEPTEMBER 1945.

the Japanese people. Not only did it bring to an end eight years of bloody warfare but it was also the first time they had heard the voice of their divine Emperor, a living God.

The first foreign invaders ever to touch Japanese soil, in the form of an advance party of US soldiers, landed at Atsugi air base near Yokohama on August 28, but the formal signing of the surrender document did not take place until September 2. The ceremony was held aboard the USS *Missouri* in Tokyo harbour with representatives of all the Allies looking on, including Generals Percival and Wainwright who had surrendered Singapore and Bataan to the Japanese three years previously. In his speech at the signing the supreme Allied commander, General MacArthur, said, "It is my earnest hope, indeed the hope of all mankind, that from this solemn occasion a better world shall emerge out of the blood and carnage of the past, a world founded upon faith and understanding, a world dedicated to the dignity of man and the fulfilment of his most cherished wish for freedom, tolerance and justice." MacArthur went on to oversee the Allied occupation of Japan and played a key role in its reconstruction; and he it was who ensured the survival of the emperor as Japan's head of state.

GENERAL MACARTHUR MAKES HIS SPEECH AT THE SIGNING OF SURRENDER ON USS *MISSOURI*.

Japan's holy war was over. From the Aleutian Islands to the coast of California, to the shores of Australia, to Ceylon and India, to China and Manchuria and thousands of islands in between, it had encompassed almost half the planet. Everywhere the destruction was enormous. In Japan itself, the major cities were almost completely destroyed; the economy lay wrecked; almost all its merchant shipping had been sunk or damaged. The numbers of dead were staggering. Estimates for China range between ten and twenty million dead, mostly civilians. Japan had lost over two million, two thirds of them military. In contrast, the American losses were just over 100,000 dead in the Pacific – and none of them civilian.

# Chapter 8

# THE RECKONING

**W**ITH THE FORMAL SURRENDER COMPLETE, THE OCCUPATION OF JAPAN BEGAN. ALTHOUGH CALLED AN ALLIED OCCUPATION, IT WAS ALMOST COMPLETELY AN AMERICAN AFFAIR, GENERAL DOUGLAS MACARTHUR EFFECTIVELY RAN JAPAN FOR THE NEXT FIVE YEARS. EARLY ON, THE RUSSIANS DEMANDED THAT JAPAN BE DIVIDED UP – AS HAD HAPPENED IN GERMANY – INTO DIFFERENT ZONES OF OCCUPATION. TO HIS CREDIT, MACARTHUR RESISTED THIS IN THE STRONGEST OF TERMS AND JAPAN REMAINED A UNITED COUNTRY.

When the US flag was first raised at the reoccupied American embassy in September 1945, MacArthur proclaimed "Have our country's flag unfurled and in Tokyo's sun let it wave in full glory as the symbol of hope for the oppressed and as a harbinger of victory for the right." To many Japanese, MacArthur became a new shogun, ruling Japan from his office on the top floor of the Dai Ichi building near the Imperial Palace in central Tokyo. One of the most memorable images of the occupation is a black and white photograph taken of MacArthur and Emperor Hirohito. MacArthur stands tall, relaxed and in charge. Hirohito looks small, awkward and uncomfortable. The victor and the defeated, side by side.

MacArthur faced a daunting task, firstly of coping with a country all but destroyed by the war, its people traumatized by defeat and literally starving in the streets. In the first winter, an average of six people a day starved to death in Tokyo alone. The newspapers were full of advertisements from people willing to swap possessions for food. Millions of families had lost their breadwinners. In addition to the dead many Japanese had been taken prisoner in the final stages of the war. The Russians alone took nearly 600,000 captives when they overran Japanese forces in Manchuria. And for those at home, Japan's cities resembled a wasteland. More than two million Japanese homes had been destroyed in US bombing raids. Japan's cities and her industrial heartland lay in ruins. In MacArthur's memoirs he recalls, "It was 22 miles from the New Grand Hotel in Yokohama to the American Embassy which was to be my home during the Occupation but they were 22 miles of devastation and vast piles of rubble." As thousands of Japanese soldiers returned from the Pacific, China and Korea, the scale of the problem grew. There were widespread shortages of all essential commodities, long food queues, refugees on the move; housing was scarce and there was sickness and disease. The black market that had existed throughout the war despite the Japanese government's efforts to eradicate it grew as a new source of illicit goods presented itself – the GIs themselves.

TOP LEFT: GENERAL MACARTHUR SETS FOOT IN JAPAN AT ATSUGI AIRBASE, AUGUST 1945.
ABOVE: THE MAIN ROAD INTO TOKYO AFTER THE SURRENDER, SEPTEMBER 1945.

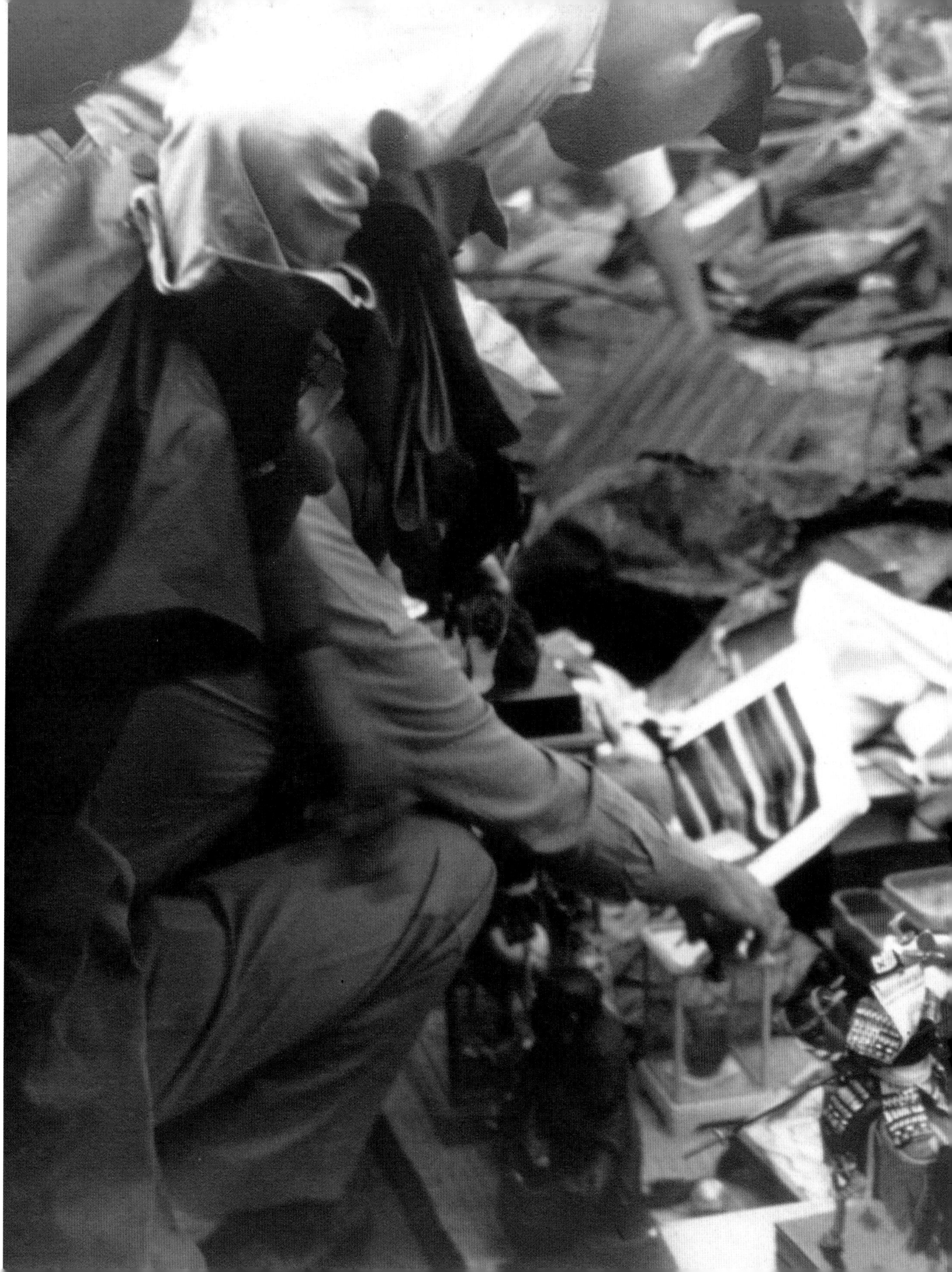

ABOVE: Japanese children waving US flags at a visit by General MacArthur, 1946.
PREVIOUS PAGE: Man selling on the Black Market in Tokyo, 1945.

Until the recent war in Iraq, the Allied occupation of Japan occupied a unique place in world history. It was the only time an occupying force had "democratised" another country by bringing in political, social and economic reforms. MacArthur had two aims in mind: firstly to dismantle and prevent the re-emergence of the militaristic regime of the 1930s that had led Japan into war; and secondly to prevent the establishment of communism amidst the ruins of Japan. As time went on and relations between the US and the USSR worsened, the second objective took precedence. Because of this, MacArthur's revolution was far from complete and many measures had been reversed by the end of the occupation in 1951.

From the start, MacArthur's authority was absolute. The terms of his office had been set out by President Truman:

> The authority of the Emperor and the Japanese government to rule the state is subordinate to you as Supreme Commander for the Allied Powers. You will exercise your authority as you deem proper to carry out your mission. Our relations with Japan do not rest on a contractual basis, but on unconditional surrender. Since your authority is supreme, you will not entertain any question on the part of the Japanese as to its scope... Control of Japan shall be exercised through the Japanese government to the extent that such an arrangement produces satisfactory results. You may enforce the orders issued to you by the employment of such measures as you deem necessary including the use of force.

MacArthur was the ideal choice for the post. He viewed himself as a man of destiny acting on the stage of history. Supremely self-confident and usually speaking in broad historical terms, he inspired the Japanese during the hard early years, giving them hope for a better future. As the occupation wore on, the Japanese had increasing respect for him.

One extraordinary aspect of the occupation was that almost from the start MacArthur's office was flooded with letters written by Japanese from all walks of life and on every subject imaginable. From all over the country, men and women, young and old, farmers, housewives, factory workers, returning soldiers, members of the communist party, even children wrote to MacArthur personally. Some were just happy the war was over and wanted to express their thanks. Others wanted help with some problem such as a lack of food or a missing son. Many complained about neighbours, the black market and taxes. Some pleaded on behalf of the emperor. Others demanded he be removed and even tried as a war criminal. Many poems were composed especially for MacArthur and letters were often beautifully written with traditional brush and ink. A few were even written in blood. One of the first letters arrived at MacArthur's office in November 1945. It was from Gompei Tsuchiya:

His Excellency General MacArthur, the stationing of your troops in Japan and political reform are great things that are welcomed by all of the Japanese people. I swear by the gods of heaven and earth my faith and gratitude for the MacArthur administration. Japanese politicians are allies of the Zaibatsu [big industrial conglomerates] and their politics are dishonest, their politics are inhumane. In my humble opinion, you should introduce great reforms of Japanese politics, remake Japan's zaibatsu through and through and return all property owned by the zaibatsu, without exception to the government. I hope you would in this manner provide food for the unemployed. There is a great mould growing on Japanese politics today ... We the people, with freedom of speech, would cleanse the mould from the souls of the politicians. We hope thereby to arrive at a reborn, cultural Japan....

By the end of the occupation MacArthur had received over half a million letters, and when he left Japan to return to the United States people were genuinely upset; there were even handwritten placards in the street displaying messages such as "We love you, General MacArthur". Aside from the genuine emotion, this was partly an indication of the relief people felt at the ending of the war and the occupation and partly a sign of the success of the occupation in preventing criticism of its own policies. Censorship of all forms of media was just as widespread during the occupation as it had been during the war. In particular, any criticism of MacArthur's policies was strictly prohibited.

AMERICAN 'PX' STORE IN TOKYO, 1945.

The Occupation did bring about some wide-ranging reforms throughout Japanese life. After the new Japanese government failed to come up with a satisfactory new constitution, MacArthur simply appointed a committee of his own made up exclusively of Americans and ordered them to come up with a draft constitution in six days. When it was complete it was handed to the Japanese, who were told to implement it without question or comment, and so a new Japanese constitution came into effect in May 1947. Both houses of the Japanese parliament were to be elected. Women were given the vote for the first time and equality of the sexes was guaranteed. Most famously, Article 9 officially outlawed war as an instrument of Japanese foreign policy. From now on Japan would have a military dedicated solely to self-defence. The occupation also witnessed extensive land reforms, extending property ownership to more people. There is no doubt that it was a radical and far-reaching overhaul of Japanese political and civil society, but for many the reforms did not go far enough.

One area of Japanese life where MacArthur resisted radical change was to the status of the emperor himself. At the beginning of the occupation Hirohito's position was very precarious. There was much popular support among the Allies, particularly in the US and Australia, for ending the imperial system in Japan and bringing Hirohito to trial. A Gallup poll in the United States discovered that more than a third of Americans wanted the emperor arrested, tried and executed as a war criminal. Only 7 per cent were prepared to leave him alone. The Soviet government also demanded the emperor be charged as a war criminal, but in contrast MacArthur saw the Emperor as a much-needed symbol of continuity and stability amid all the radical changes. He was convinced that should Hirohito be brought to trial, the Allies would face a Japanese uprising and possibly guerrilla warfare. The emperor featured in a chilling letter MacArthur received in December 1945. It had been written in blood:

> To the honourable General MacArthur, I respectfully petition: Please exclude His Majesty the emperor from responsibility for the war. For us Japanese, His Majesty is absolute, and he is the life of the Japanese people. If Your Excellency contemplates the future of Japan and desires true peace in the world, you will realize that a policy of leaving His Majesty in place in Japan is advantageous not for Japan alone. If it ever happens that His Majesty is brought to trial, not only I but many Japanese, whose loyalty is close to a religious belief that has deepened through history and tradition, would hold a tremendous hatred not only toward you, but toward all Americans forever... I swear to God that I am willing to offer my life. Please understand my humble feelings.

The emperor was spared a trial and remained on the Chrysanthemum Throne, but all power was stripped from him. Under the new constitution he remained at the head of Japanese life but merely as "the symbol of the state and of the unity of the people, deriving his position from the will of the people with whom resides sovereign power". The emperor also "voluntarily" gave up his divine status in a statement on New Year's Day 1946.

Perhaps the occupation's greatest mistake was its failure to complete the reform of Japanese politics. While all elements of militarism were eradicated and a new more democratic constitution brought in, the all-powerful government bureaucracy remained largely untouched. It was here that the forces of conservatism were strongest and it was here that real power resided. In this major area Japan was unchanged and many of the same people remained in power. As time went on, MacArthur's early radicalism slowly evaporated. Although he re-established trade unions allowing membership to balloon from zero to over 3.5 million by 1947, when a general strike was called to protest at low wages MacArthur ordered the army to stop it spreading. The Cold War had begun and the Americans were taking no chances. The early ideals of the occupation gradually faded away. The break-up of the huge industrial conglomerates that had done so much to fuel the militarism of the 1930s was halted. Instead they were reformed and renamed *Keiretsu*, and so began a new Japanese conquest of the world, this time by economic means. Within 30 years Japan had transformed itself from a defeated, shattered nation into the world's second most powerful economy. Japan had conquered the world at last, but this time by peaceful means.

CHILD IN THE RUINS OF TOKYO, 1945.

With surrender came the inevitable reckoning after years of brutal warfare, and the Allies had a long list of wanted war criminals. The first Japanese to be convicted and executed for war crimes was General Tomoyuki Yamashita, the "Lion of Singapore". He was tried by a commission of five generals, all American, sitting in the ballroom of the war-damaged US High Commissioner's residence in Manila. Yamashita's crime was not that he personally had done anything illegal, but that officers and men under his command had committed atrocities including murder. Yamashita's counsel at the trial described his predicament:

> The Accused is not charged with having done something or having failed to do something, but solely with having been something ... American jurisprudence recognizes no such principle so far as its own military personnel are concerned ... No one would even suggest that the Commanding General of an American occupational force becomes a criminal every time an American soldier violates the law ... one man is not held to answer for the crime of another.

But Yamashita was.

In the last days of the Japanese occupation of Manila in the Philippines his troops had gone on a rampage of torture, rape and slaughter, including the murder of women, children, priests and American POWs. Neither side disputed that the events had taken place, but in the eyes of the prosecution Yamashita must have known about them and should have done more to stop them. They refused to accept the argument that all law and order, normal military communication and discipline had broken down and that Yamashita was no longer in control of his own men.

The prosecution case was pushed to its logical conclusion. Despite an appeal, the judgement was that Yamashita was guilty as charged. Interestingly the verdict was handed down on December 7, 1945, four years to the day after Pearl Harbor. He was hanged in Manila on February 23, 1946. Yamashita was just one of thousands of Japanese soldiers brought to book for their actions during the war and for crimes stretching back to events in China in the 1930s. Throughout the war, the Allies had given repeated warnings that they would seek out and prosecute war criminals once the fighting was over. The most direct threat emerged from the Potsdam conference in July 1945, when it was announced that "there must be eliminated for all time the authority and influence of those who have deceived and misled the people of Japan into embarking on world conquest ... Stern justice must be meted out to all war criminals, including those who have visited cruelties upon our prisoners ..."

Japanese leaders were tried in Tokyo by the International Military Tribunal for the Far East. It started proceedings in May 1946 and was presided over by representatives of each of the Allied powers – the United States, Great Britain, Australia, the Netherlands, France, Canada, India, New Zealand, the Soviet Union, the Philippines and China. Since the United States had borne more than the lion's share of the fighting, the other Allies were content to let the Americans take the lead in the prosecutions.

From the beginning, the Allies agreed on one basic principle: that the trials should be held in public and thus be seen to be fair. Both the world and Japan itself must be shown how justly the victors of this war could deal with war crimes. The charter under which the Tokyo court operated gave it jurisdiction over persons accused of offences that included the somewhat difficult to define "crimes against peace", as well as "conspiracy to wage aggressive war" and "crimes against humanity". There were two glaring omissions in this attempt to cleanse Japan. Firstly, none of the zaibatsu was ever investigated; secondly, nor was the emperor: his name was never mentioned during the trials.

In total, there were 28 defendants, two of whom died during the proceedings, while a third became so mentally ill that he could no longer stand trial. They had all been officials of the highest rank in the Japanese government: four had been prime ministers; there were also four former foreign ministers, five war ministers, two navy ministers and four ambassadors. Fourteen had been former army generals and three had been admirals in the navy.

They faced a list of 55 charges, including 36 crimes against peace, 16 charges of murder and three charges of "other conventional war crimes and crimes against humanity". In brief, they were accused of conspiring between 1928 and 1945 to wage "aggressive war" to bring about a Japanese "domination and control of East Asia".

[146

T
H
E

R
E
C
K
O
N
I
N
G

The prosecution opened its case in May 1946 following an opening speech from Sir William Webb in which he said, "To our great task we bring open minds both on the facts and the law. The onus will be on the prosecution to establish guilt beyond a reasonable doubt." The makeshift courtroom had been set up in the former war ministry in Ichigaya. Both press and public were present – even film cameras were allowed – as detailed statements from over 1,200 witnesses and thousands of documents were laid before the court.

One serious problem the defendants and their lawyers faced was the lack of an effective system of simultaneous translation from English to Japanese and vice versa. As a result they were restricted to brief questioning in simple language or the use of written questions submitted beforehand.

The trial ended after more than two years in November 1948 but it was another seven months before the verdicts were announced. All the defendants were found guilty. For seven – former Prime Minister Tojo, former Foreign Minister Koki Hirota and five generals (Doihara, Itagaki, Kimura, Matsui and Muto) – the sentence was death by hanging. Of the rest, 16 got life imprisonment and only two were given lighter sentences of several years apiece. Of the judges, four disagreed in various minor ways with the final judgement. Only one judge dissented completely. Radhabinod Pal of recently independent India claimed that the defendants should be acquitted of all charges; that their actions had been based wholly on self-defence forced on Japan by severe economic pressure from the Allies. He dismissed Japanese atrocities as "stray incidents". Pal had been a member of the Indian National Army that had fought alongside the Japanese against the British in Burma. He became a hero of the Japanese right wing and continues to fuel their revisionist fantasies.

Of all the evidence submitted, the most damning was the extent to which Japan had consistently violated the laws of warfare. Compared to the Germans and Italians, whose treatment of Allied POWs had resulted in the deaths of only four per cent of those captured, the Japanese had caused the death of over 31 per cent of those prisoners captured during the course of the Pacific War, who had died through disease, mistreatment, malnutrition and cold-blooded murder.

The Tokyo tribunal presided over only a tiny proportion of the total of war crimes trials, which continued into the early 1950s. Former Japanese soldiers and government officials were put on trial all over the Far East, accused of "lesser" crimes such as rape, murder and the brutal treatment of prisoners and civilians. Nineteen Japanese military doctors were tried for performing hideous experiments on the island of Truk in 1944. They were found guilty of murdering American POWs by injecting them with virulent strains of bacteria. A former Japanese vice admiral and ten others were found guilty of murdering 98 Pan American airline employees on Wake Island in 1943, for which they were all sentenced to death. Another group of 18 Japanese soldiers was convicted of murdering civilians in the Palau Islands.

The most publicized of the British trials was the prosecution of the River Kwai defendants, those who had caused the deaths of more than 16,000 prisoners forced to build the Burma–Siam railroad. The two worst offenders were hanged, the rest given long prison sentences. The Australian trials uncovered some of the worst crimes. One court in New Guinea found a Japanese officer guilty of cannibalism, for eating part of an Australian POW. He was hanged. Another found a Japanese guilty of the crucifixion of four airmen in the Celebes Islands. He was also hanged. In yet another the Australians found a total of 93 Japanese soldiers guilty of the same crime. They had forced more than 1,000 Dutch, Australian and American POWs to make a 165-mile march from which only 183 survived. A further 150 died in the next few days and the Japanese commander had then murdered the few survivors. He was executed. The Chinese tried over 800 Japanese defendants, including some who had taken part in the infamous Rape of Nanking. Five hundred were found guilty and 149 executed.

In one of the most distressing trials in the Dutch East Indies former Vice Admiral Kamada was found guilty of ordering the execution of more than 1,500 tribesmen in Borneo. He was hanged. The Dutch also executed four other Japanese for brutality and murder involving 2,000 Dutch prisoners on Flores Island. A handful of Japanese defendants actually admitted their crimes. One former camp commander described how he had tortured prisoners by gouging out their eyes; another former Kempei Tai officer was even prepared to show the court how he had viciously kicked a prisoner. The Russian trials were probably the most bizarre, and were largely used for propaganda attacks on the West. With the Cold War already underway, the Russian continually pointed out how the Americans had failed to bring the *zaibatsu* to justice.

The last trial was heard in 1951 and by that stage more than 5,600 Japanese had been prosecuted in over 2,200 different trials and over 4,400 had been convicted, of whom about 1,000 were executed. United States Supreme Court Justice Murphy summed up the problems faced by the imposition of victors' justice: "Justice had to be preserved, no matter what the cost, no matter what guilty men went free ... To conclude otherwise, is to admit that the enemy has lost the battle but has destroyed our ideals." With the benefit of hindsight, one error made by the Allies was the complete lack of a Japanese presence on any of the tribunals. There were many people in Japan who would have welcomed playing a part in the prosecution of those who had been responsible for the horrors of the 1930s and 1940s; such a move might have helped the long-term process of exorcising the demons of those years.

VICE ADMIRAL MICHITORO TOTSUKA SURRENDERS AT YOKOSUKA NAVAL BASE, AUGUST 1945.

# THE DARK SHADOW OF HISTORY

**T**HE SECOND WORLD WAR CONTINUES TO CAST A DARK SHADOW OVER THE JAPANESE PEOPLE, AND JAPAN HAS DONE LITTLE TO EXORCISE ITS DEMONS. GERMANY HAS GONE A LONG WAY TO EXPIATING THE EVIL OF THE NAZI ERA WITH OFFICIAL APOLOGIES, LAWS AGAINST HOLOCAUST DENIAL, FUNDS TO COMPENSATE THE FAMILIES OF PEOPLE MURDERED AND SO ON. THERE HAS BEEN NO OFFICIAL ATTEMPT TO EXCUSE WHAT HAPPENED AND EVERY EFFORT MADE TO MAKE AMENDS. IN JAPAN, ALMOST THE COMPLETE OPPOSITE IS TRUE. THERE HAVE BEEN FEW OFFICIAL APOLOGIES, ONLY GRUDGINGLY GIVEN "EXPLANATIONS" EVEN THEN ONLY AFTER INTENSE INTERNATIONAL PRESSURE.

There has been no official condemnation of right-wing revisionist histories about the war and whenever the question of compensation – for POWs brutalized or Korean comfort women forced into prostitution – is raised, the Japanese government simply points to the San Francisco peace treaty of 1952, which it claims effectively closed the door to any further claims. Perhaps most important of all, the Japanese have never held their own war crimes trials to root out the evil committed in the Emperor's name from 1931 to 1945. In Japan the war is still a very raw subject and not just for the generation that fought it.

Perhaps the most potentially damaging legacy of the war is how it continues to be taught in schools. In Germany there is absolutely no ambiguity about the horrors and crimes of the Nazi era; they were undeniably evil and wrong – and by implication must never happen again – and the school textbooks say so. In Japan, the story is less clear. In 2001, Prime Minister Junichiro Koizumi provoked a diplomatic rift with South Korea and China over a school history textbook that attempted to sanitize and justify the role of Japanese militarism in Asia in the first half of the twentieth century. In April of that year, the disputed book was approved for use in high schools despite South Korean historians pointing out 25 passages or omissions that distorted the history of Japan's occupation of Korea from 1905 to 1945. Chinese academics singled out another eight passages or omissions that distorted the Japanese seizure of Manchuria in 1931 and the war in China from 1937 to 1945.

The text had been written by a revisionist academic group called the History Textbook Reform Society, formed in January 1997. By 2001 it claimed to have over 10,000 members, including several hundred top politicians and leading figures in the business world. It was clearly a powerful and well funded group. Along with the rest of Japan's resurgent right wing, it believed that the history of the war had been hijacked by the victors and that over the years the Japanese people had taken a masochistic delight in agreeing with this version. Their argument for the revision of history was largely based on Japan's current economic woes. With the post-war economic miracle at an end and after ten years of recession, they argued that Japan needed revitalizing, and a key part of that process was to instil renewed pride in the nation's past among the young.

The society's website boldly stated that the Americans had "expunged Japan's history, injecting in its place a history fabricated by the victors. Japan became the source of all evils in accounts of wars subsequent to the Manchurian Incident." The society argued that Japan had gone to war in both China and the Pacific to defend itself against encirclement by the Western colonial powers, and that this explains and excuses all Japan's subsequent actions, including by implication all the atrocities in the 1930s and 1940s. It even denied certain atrocities took place and pointed to the US firebombing campaign of 1945 and the decision to drop two A-bombs on civilian targets with the consequent enormous loss of life as a

Japanese troops capture Shanghai, August 1937.

# The Scholar's Bookshelf

110 Melrich Road • Cranbury, NJ 08512 • Tel (609) 395-6933 • Fax (609) 395-0755

Dear Customer:

Thank you for your order. If you are an academic the following information may be of interest to you:

1.  You can obtain copies in quantity for classroom use by either ordering directly from us or through your college bookstore. Bookstores must order directly from us to receive the sale prices, as copies are still available from the original publishers at the full prices.

2.  If you wish to circulate this catalog to graduate students (we do not reach them directly), additional copies in quantity can be sent to you or your department.

3.  If you have the responsibility for recommending books for your departmental or central library, you may want to use the catalog attached, or request another copy.

Sincerely,

Geri Johnson

rmw

sign of US and Allied war guilt, the intention being to excuse the crimes of imperial Japan by pointing the finger at its enemies.

Nanjing and the events surrounding its capture in December 1937 are key to the society's revisionist argument and to similar attempts in Japan to refashion its recent history. There is undeniable evidence that the Japanese invasion of China from 1937 onwards was marked by particular barbarity. At least ten million Chinese civilians and 1.3 million soldiers were killed between 1937 and 1945 but the textbook initially omitted any reference at all to the Nanjing massacre when maybe as many as a quarter of a million Chinese soldiers and civilians were butchered. After an international outcry, there is now a mention of the massacre in the revised school textbook but it is simply referred to as the "Nanjing Incident" and is described only as being "the subject of debate". The international row over the textbook became so bitter that Korea threatened to recall its ambassador from Tokyo and two Japanese navy ships were refused permission to dock in Inchon. In the end, schools themselves largely refused to adopt the textbook. But the fact that the dispute involved the government and not some right-wing fringe group makes it all the more worrying.

The battle over the truth about Japan's military past is bound up with her economic future. The present administration's power base, as with almost all Japan's post-war governments, is essentially right wing, and part of its strategy to revive Japan's economic fortunes includes reviving a sense of national pride. Also relevant is pressure to revise Japan's pacifist constitution and to rewrite the famous Article 9, which permits only a military force dedicated to the nation's self-defence and prohibits one that can operate abroad in an offensive capacity. The government's desire to revoke this clause and revive Japan as a military power has a large amount of popular support.

Such sentiments are found throughout Japanese civil and political society today. The mayor of Tokyo, Shintaro Ishihara, has consistently spoken out against Japanese war guilt in the most inflammatory way, and he is clearly a popular figure as he was recently re-elected with a large majority. Over the last six years, the Fuji-Sankei communications empire, the owner of some of Japan's largest television and radio stations and its fifth largest newspaper, *Sankei Shimbun*, has given much editorial space and support to the History Textbook Reform Society and similar right-wing groups. Moreover, successive prime ministers have provoked international con-troversy by visiting and worshipping at the Yasukuni shrine on August 15, the anniversary of Japan's surrender.

There is an alternative view within Japan but it lacks the power and presence of the right wing. Its strongest proponent was the historian Professor Saburo Ienaga. In the early 1960s Professor Ienaga was employed by the government to write a school history textbook. The completed work contained references to the infamous Unit 731. The Japanese government has never officially acknowledged the unit's existence, so it censored the references. Ienaga began a protracted series of court cases to prove that this was illegal. After 32 years of legal wrangles, he finally won his case in September 1997, in the supreme court in Tokyo. However, the court ruled that only some of the censored references be reinstated and it also upheld the government's right to edit future school textbooks. The long legal battle and the criticism from the right had taken its toll and Professor Ienaga died of heart failure in December 2002. No one has yet emerged to continue his struggle.

Government-supported efforts to legitimize the history and symbols of Japanese militarism could be seen as the first move in an aggressive reassertion of Japanese imperialism in Asia and elsewhere, a return to the dark days of the 1930s and 1940s. For years, the right wing in Japan has been relatively quiet. Its only obvious – at least to outsiders – manifestation is the regular parade of the black-painted sound trucks which roam the streets of Tokyo on certain days of the year, blasting out patriotic speeches and wartime songs. Most people in Japan think of them as a joke, but they are beginning to seem more sinister, the tip of a right-wing iceberg which is growing bigger. In recent years, those who

JAPANESE SOLDIER IN FRONT OF THE GRAVES OF FELLOW SOLDIERS IN MALAYA, 1942.

have fallen foul of right wingers have rued the day. There are now thought to be more than 800 extreme right-wing groups in Japan with over 100,000 members. Many have strong links with Japan's version of the mafia, the *yakuza*. Like the armed militia movement in the US, these groups live in a world of paranoid conspiracies with their country as the victim. Their beliefs are

A Japanese fighter pilot from 1944.

racist and hate-filled and they are prepared to resort to violence and terrorism. A fleet of sound trucks appeared outside the headquarters of the Softbank Corporation in 1997 and broadcast round-the-clock abuse of the most threatening kind against its president. They objected to the fact that Softbank had US partners. When the head of the Japanese Democratic Party went to Korea and said that Japan should take more responsibility over the issue of comfort women, the sound trucks surrounded his house, their loudspeakers blaring, "Hatoyama, kill yourself! Hatoyama, resign! Hatoyama! Kill! Kill! Hatoyama! Smash him to Death!" In recent years right-wing extremists have taken shots at a prime minister, wounded two leading Japanese MPs, firebombed Japan's parliament building, taken journalists hostage and attacked several prominent people they considered enemies of Japan.

The creed of most right-wing societies is frighteningly similar to those of the groups that spearheaded Japan's march to militarism in the 1920s. They believe that Japan has become too much like the West and has lost many of the things that make it unique. They believe that the emperor system should be strengthened; that schoolchildren should be made to sing the national anthem; that everyone should be proud of the flag that flew over Japan's soldiers in the Second World War. Just like their predecessors 70 or 80 years ago, they blame politicians and businessmen for having got Japan in such a mess. They have names such as the Association to Save the Nation and Encourage the Cause or the Great Japan Sincerity Association. They have mottoes like "One assassination saves millions of lives." One of the main groups, the Japan Alliance, has had two presidents who were involved in political assassinations in the 1930s. A more recent leader, Hiroki Ooto, has publicly stated he would not hesitate to do the same.

In May 1998, a new and highly controversial Japanese film about the war years had its premiere in Tokyo. It was called simply *Pride* and its hero was Hideki Tojo, Japan's wartime leader and executed war criminal. The film deals with Tojo's trial and portrays him as a Japanese patriot who was unjustly treated by the victorious Allies. It relates how throughout this process, right up to the moment of his execution, Tojo maintained his pride in both himself and his country. On the subject of Nanjing, the film gives much emphasis to Tojo's remarks that, "All evidence is only hearsay evidence, which doesn't deserve to be called evidence. Moreover, it is an exaggeration, and worse,

some has been completely fabricated. Who could believe that they [Japan's soldiers] would carry out indiscriminate killing, and kill even women and children at random. They are soldiers of the Japanese Imperial Army." The film made over $169 million at the box office in its first year in Japan.

*Pride* was based on a book written by Tojo's grand-daughter, Yuko Iwanami, who is leading moves to revive his memory, not as a war criminal, but as a Japanese patriot. She even made a well-publicized visit to the USS *Arizona* memorial at Pearl Harbor in an attempt to gain international recognition for her efforts to rehabilitate the memory of her grandfather. Along with the rest of the right wing she argues that her grandfather had no choice but to go to war. By late 1941 Japan's very survival was threatened by the US oil embargo, which she describes as a jealous attempt by the larger Western powers to strangle an emerging Asian rival. She complains that the image of her grandfather as a butcher responsible for the deaths of millions in China and elsewhere in the Pacific was largely a fabrication of the Tokyo war trials, which she says wrongfully sentenced him and six other Japanese leaders to death. The fact that she can say these things in public without government condemnation is a huge victory for the right in Japan and a sign of its growing power.

In contrast to the film about Tojo, only a handful of Japanese cinemas dared to show *Nanjing 1937*, a Chinese film released at the same time detailing the atrocities committed by Japanese soldiers after the capture of the city. Right-wing protesters invaded one of the cinemas in Tokyo where it was being shown and slashed the screen.

For many Japanese, the war years were a dark period in their history that brought intense suffering and pain to their neighbours in Asia and around the Pacific. But there is also a growing number who believe that the period was not one of which Japan should be ashamed but one in which the nation's imperial dream almost came to fruition. It was a time of glorious deeds, of heroic battles and patriotic sacrifices; it was not a time of evil but Japan's finest hour and should now be the inspiration for a new generation.

For Japan, the war with the West that began with the first tentative encounters in the mid-nineteenth century is still being fought today. The killing may have stopped but the battle to establish the truth goes on. And until it ends the memory of Japan's war cannot be laid to rest.

## BIBLIOGRAPHY:

Noel Barber – *Sinister Twilight: The Fall of Singapore* (London 1968)
Ian Buruma – *The Wages of Guilt* (London 1994)
Iris Chang – *The Rape of Nanking* (New York 1997)
Haruko Taya Cook & Theodore F. Cook – *Japan at War: An Oral History* (New York 1992)
John Dower – *War Without Mercy* (New York 1986)
John Dower – *Embracing Defeat* (London 1999)
Ed. David C. Evans – *The Japanese Navy in World War Two* (Maryland 1969)
Richard B. Frank – *Downfall: The End of the Imperial Japanese Empire* (New York 1999)
Mitsuo Fuchida & Masatake Okumiya – *Midway: The Japanese Story* (London 2002)
Robert Guillain – *I Saw Tokyo Burning* (London 1981)
Isoko and Ichiro Hatano – *Mother and Son: A Wartime Correspondence* (Boston 1962)
Thomas R. Havens – *Valley of Darkness: The Japanese People and World War Two* (New York 1986)
Lt. Commander Tota Ishimaru – *Japan Must Fight Britain* (London 1936)
Masuo Kato – *The Lost War* (New York 1946)
Okakura Kakuzo – *The Awakening of Japan* (New York 1904)
Ruth Ann Keyso – *Women of Okinawa* (New York 2000)
Kiyosawa Kiyoshi, trans. By Eugene Soviak – *A Diary of Darkness* (New Jersey 1999)
Ryuji Nagatsuka – *I Was A Kamikaze* (New York 1972)
Hiroko Nakamoto – *My Japan 1930–1951* (New York 1970)
Tetsuro Ogawa – *Terraced Hell* (Vermont 1972)
Toyofumi Ogura – *Letters From The End of the World* (Tokyo 1982)
The Pacific War Research Society – *Japan's Longest Day* (Tokyo 1968)
Erna Paris – Long Shadows: Truth, Lies and History (London 2001)
Saburo Sakai with Martin Caidin & Fred Saito – *Samurai* (New York 1957)
Sadako Sawamura – *My Asakusa* (Boston 2000)
Ed. Sangmie Choi Schellstede – *Comfort Women Speak* (New York 2000)
Ooka Shohei – *Taken Captive* (New York 1996)
Rinjiro Sodei – *Dear General MacArthur* (Maryland 2001)
Kazuo Tamayama & John Nunneley – *Tales by Japanese Soldiers* (London 2000)
John Toland – *The Rising Sun* (London 2001)
Colonel Masanobu Tsuji – *Japan's Greatest Victory. Britain's Worst Defeat* (New York 1993)
Ryusaku Tsunoda, Wm. Theodore De Bary, Donald Keene – *Sources of Japanese Tradition, Vol II* (New York 1958)
Ann Waswo – *Modern Japanese Society 1868–1994* (Oxford 1996)
Dick Wilson – *When Tigers Fight* (London 1982)
Colonel Hiromichi Yahara – *The Battle for Okinawa* (New York 1995)
Midori Yamanouchi and Joseph L. Quinn – *Listen to The Voices from the Sea* (Scranton 2000)
Tsuneta Yano & Kyoichi Shirasaki – *Nippon: A Charted Survey of Japan 1936* (Tokyo 1936)

## PICTURE CREDITS: